THE FORGOTTEN CONTRIBUTION OF THE TEACHING SISTERS

STUDIA PAEDAGOGICA

New Series
44

Editorial Board
Prof. Dr. M. Depaepe (Chairman)
Prof. Dr. B. Maes
Prof. Dr. A. De Munter
Prof. Dr. G. Kelchtermans
Prof. Dr. J. Vandenabeele (Secretary)

Studia Paedagogica

THE FORGOTTEN CONTRIBUTION OF THE TEACHING SISTERS

A HISTORIOGRAPHICAL ESSAY ON THE EDUCATIONAL WORK OF CATHOLIC WOMEN RELIGIOUS IN THE 19TH AND 20TH CENTURIES

Bart Hellinckx, Frank Simon & Marc Depaepe

LEUVEN UNIVERSITY PRESS

© 2009 Leuven University Press / Universitaire Pers Leuven / Presses Universitaires de Louvain, Minderbroedersstraat 4, B-3000 Leuven

All rights reserved. Except in those cases expressly determined by law, no part of this publication may be multiplied, saved in an automated datafile or made public in any way whatsoever without the express prior written consent of the publishers.

ISBN 978 90 5867 765 5

D / 2009 / 1869 / 40

NUR: 849

Contents

Acknowledgements

We would first like to thank the Flemish union of teachers *Christelijk Onderwijzers Verbond* (COV) and its Secretary General, Romain Maes, for giving the first author the chance to undertake this research as part of a broader historical study of women in teaching and the teachers' union.

We are also particularly grateful to the department of Education and Training of the Flemish government and the confederation of Christian unions in Belgium *Algemeen Christelijk Vakverbond* (ACV) for awarding the project a grant. These grants not only helped us to cover part of the additional research expenses, they also enabled the first author to attend several conferences in Belgium and abroad. Preliminary results of the study were presented at the workshop entitled 'Christian Feminisation and Masculinisation in Europe: Comparative Perspectives' in Ghent (5th January 2008), the Seventh European Social Science History Conference in Lisbon (26th February 2008) and the 15th International Congress of the *Asociación de Historiadores Latinoamericanistas Europeos* (AHILA) in Leiden (27th August 2008).

We would further like to thank Marjet Derks, Marit Monteiro and Kristien Suenens for sharing with us some important information on publications, research projects and conferences. Likewise, we are grateful to Jan De Maeyer and Annemieke van Drenth for their interesting remarks and suggestions.

We also thank all our colleagues in the research unit on the history of education at the KU.Leuven, the *Centrum voor Historische Pedagogiek*. They always followed the progress of the research with great interest and offered useful comments during an internal research seminar.

Last but not least, a special word of gratitude goes to Lies Van Rompaey. Although she was primarily involved in her own part of the wider research project, the presence 'in the background' of this jovial, inspiring and supporting colleague contributed significantly to the successful outcome of the undertaking.

Chapter 1

Introduction

Background of the research

While we were studying the process of the feminization of the teaching profession in Belgium in the 19th and 20th centuries as part of a research project of the Flemish teachers' union *Christelijk Onderwijzers Verbond* (COV) and the sections on history of education of the *Katholieke Universiteit Leuven* and the *Universiteit Gent*,[1] we noticed that the extensive international literature on the feminization of teaching focuses almost exclusively on the influx of lay women into teaching.[2] This observation made us wonder what is known about the women religious who entered teaching in huge numbers during the 19th and 20th centuries.

Searching for a general overview of the historical research on women religious teachers, we came across only three articles which contain some useful historiographical information on the subject: an essay review by F. Michael Perko on religious schooling in America,[3] a historiographical essay by Tom O'Donoghue and Anthony Potts on both male and female teaching orders in the English-speaking world,[4] and an article on the historiography of girls' education in France by Rebecca Rogers.[5]

The lack of a broad overview of the historical research on women religious teachers contrasts markedly with the relatively large number of reviews of the literature on the history of women religious in general.[6] Convinced that a better knowledge of the involvement of women religious in education might open up new avenues of research into the complex process of the feminization of teaching, we decided to review the historiography of the teaching sisters.

Scope

Because women from several religious denominations contributed to education in widely varying ways, in a vast geographical area and over a long period of time, it was necessary to limit our review in a number of ways. We chose to focus exclusively on Catholic women religious and to pay no attention to, for example, the contribution of the Anglican sisterhoods.[7] We also restricted our study to the 19th and 20th centuries, the 'Age of the Teaching Congregations',[8] leaving aside the relatively well-studied educational work which several orders undertook from the 16th to the 18th century.[9] Geographically, we have decided to include only North America, Latin America, Australasia (Australia and New Zealand) and ten Western European countries (Austria, Belgium, France, Germany, Great Britain, Ireland, the Netherlands, Portugal, Spain and Switzerland).

Our survey does not cover the whole spectrum of educational activities: colonial or missionary education provided by European Catholic orders in Africa and Asia has not been touched.[10] Likewise, the contribution of such orders to the field of educational sciences falls outside the scope of the present study.[11]

As the title of our study indicates, we are focussing particularly on the involvement of women religious in education. Aspects such as the place of these women in the Church, their spiritual and communal life, the balance of power within these groups, their internal organization, their femininity, their contribution to the women's movement, etc., will not be taken into account unless they have a direct bearing on educational matters.

To narrow down the number of publications to be included in our survey further, we have restricted ourselves to an assessment of the literature which appeared between 1985 and 2009.

Our focus is on published materials, i.e. books and articles; unpublished theses have generally not been taken into account.[12] Because the papers delivered at conferences are often a good indicator of the topics and approaches which are in vogue in a particular research field, a special effort has been made to include the conference papers of which at least an abstract was available, especially those of the important 'International Standing Conference for the History of Education' (ISCHE).

Since one of our goals is to determine the degree of attention which the subject has received in the field of the history of education, special emphasis is placed on articles published in research journals of that discipline, as well as on books reviewed in those journals. Twenty periodicals devoted to the history of education were thoroughly screened.[13] Although the articles and books identified in this way form the core of the literature discussed here, many other relevant publications were also taken into account.

Aims and objectives

Our aim is to determine the state of the research conducted on the involvement of women religious in education in the last twenty-five years. Which aspects have been examined in detail and which topics have hardly been touched upon? What are the key theories, concepts and ideas? What are the major issues and debates about the topic? Which approaches have been followed? What are the main methodologies and research techniques which have been used? Can one recognize an evolution in the way researchers have looked at these women?

In our survey we also want to determine the place which the study of these women currently occupies in the field of the history of education, and we want to demonstrate the absolute need for further research on these women teachers. In order to stimulate and guide such new research, we will indicate which (sub)themes need more study and which approaches, angles and methods may be useful.

Further, we hope that this broad overview of the international literature will advance comparisons between individual teaching congregations, between congregations in different countries, and between the educational activities of Catholic women religious on the one hand and the educational work of lay women teachers, non-Catholic women religious educators, and male religious teachers on the other hand.

Finally, it is hoped that the material provided by this essay will ultimately contribute to a better understanding of the complex process of the feminization of teaching.

Organization of the study

The core of the study consists of two parts. The first part, Chapter 2, outlines the evolution of scholarly interest in the educational work of women religious.

First, we address the long-standing neglect and marginalization of the topic. Next, we describe how women religious eventually became a subject worthy of historical study and how historians of education at last also started to realize the importance of the subject. Finally, we review the proposals made by a number of scholars to renew the historiography of the sisters' involvement in educational matters. The second part, Chapter 3, surveys and assesses the literature on six major themes connected with the involvement of teaching sisters in education: (1) contribution to schooling, (2) teaching orders and schools, (3) educational philosophy, content and practice, (4) life and the lived experience of teachers and students, (5) the professionalization of teaching, and (6) changes in the composition of the teaching staff. The book ends with some general conclusions and an extensive bibliography.

Throughout the study we will use the terms 'order' and 'congregation' interchangeably, as well as 'nun' and 'sister'. Canonically speaking, sisters take simple vows and live in congregations, whereas nuns take solemn vows and live in cloistered orders.

CHAPTER 2

Evolution of scholarly interest in the educational work of women religious

A tale of historical neglect and marginalization

Historians from Europe, Australia and the Americas have observed that the involvement of women religious in education has hardly been studied hitherto.[14] Elizabeth Smyth in 2006 called them "a marginalized cohort of educators".[15] In a *status quaestionis* of educational historiography in Europe Marie-Madeleine Compère noted that the teaching profession is usually associated with the lay woman teacher.[16] That disproportionate attention is paid to lay educators appears clearly from Isabelle Havelange's evaluation of the bibliography regarding the history of education in France which is published annually in a separate issue of the journal *Histoire de l'Éducation*: in 1995, the studies about religious teachers (both women and men) made up only 13% of all publications about school personnel.[17] In his assessment of the history of education at the end of the second millennium, Jurgen Herbst noted that scholars traditionally tend to focus on public education and largely ignore private schooling.[18] Since the sisters worked to a large extent in the private sector, their work has automatically fallen outside the scope of most of the research which has been conducted.

Our literature review confirms that the educational contribution of women religious has received only limited scholarly attention so far. Not a single journal issue has been devoted to this subject and specific conferences about women religious and education seem to be very scarce. Excluding a French conference on teaching sisters of the 16th to 20th centuries which took place as long ago as 1980,[19] we are aware only of the symposium on religious communities and education which was held at the University of Laval in Quebec in 2004, and even this conference was not exclusively devoted to the contribution of the female orders.[20]

Biographical dictionaries of educationists rarely cover women religious. A famous biographical compendium which briefly describes the lives and work of more than 500 Americans, Canadians and Europeans who have played significant roles in shaping the modern western traditions of education, contains a single entry about a sister![21]

The study of women teachers focuses largely on the lay woman teacher. The two most important collective studies on the history of women teachers do not contain a single contribution on teaching sisters;[22] group biographies about women teachers tend to ignore women religious,[23] and, as was already pointed out in the introduction, historical studies on the feminization of the teaching staff usually do not deal with the massive influx of women religious teachers, but focus on the increase in lay women teachers in public schools.[24]

Since women religious are almost consistently ignored when a particular aspect of women teachers is studied, the literature on their contribution to education is only a fraction of that which exists on lay women teachers and the state of research is far less advanced.[25]

The limited scholarly attention to sisters in the field of the history of education is not an isolated phenomenon, but part of the long-standing neglect of women religious by historians. Caitriona Clear put it clearly in her book about women religious in 19th century Ireland: "Nuns have suffered the fate of historical marginalisation".[26]

The discovery of women religious as a historical 'subject'

In 1985 a reviewer of Claude Langlois's study *Le catholicisme au féminin* pointed out that the author had succeeded magnificently in 'inventing' and 'transforming' the 'good sisters' into a subject for scientific investigation.[27] The work was indeed exceptional for its size and the depth of its scholarship, and it did certainly lift the study of women religious to a much higher level. However, to label this work as the birth certificate of the scientific study of Catholic women religious would be a step too far. Whereas the historiography of religious institutes was originally the work of industrious members of the religious orders themselves, it became a more scholarly enterprise around 1950 when much of the historical research was carried out by university-educated members of religious institutes and by professional historians not directly associated with such institutes. In the 1970s scholarly interest in both the institutes and the women religious grew considerably, partly as a consequence of developments in historical science such as the emergence of women's history in the 1970s, and certainly also as a result of Vatican Council II (1962-1965). Not only urged the 'Decree on the adaptation and renewal of religious life' (*Perfectae Caritatis*) the religious institutes to adjust to the changed conditions of our time, it also asked them to return to their original spirit, and this made them delve into their own history or ask professional historians to do so.[28]

By the beginning of the third millennium the study of women religious had developed into a separate and almost fully-grown research field with national and international research groups, conferences, literature reviews, websites, special journal issues, etc.[29] Next to Langlois's fundamental study on the explosive growth of women's congregations in 19th century France, many important 'national' or 'regional' syntheses about women religious in the 19th and 20th centuries have appeared in the last twenty years.[30]

In the wake of the blossoming of studies on women religious and as a side effect of the growing attention to the history of women's education since the 1980s,[31] historians of education are beginning to explore the work of women religious. This can be most clearly deduced from the increasing number of publications devoted to the subject. As thirty-one out of the thirty-six articles about women religious which appeared between 1985 and 2009 in the twenty history of education periodicals examined by us were published after 1993, it seems that around that time historians of education started to pay more attention to these neglected women teachers.

That there is a growing interest in the topic appears for example also from a doctorate on the educational project of Teresa de Saldanha, the foundress of the Portuguese teaching congregation *Irmãs Dominicanas de Santa Catarina de Sena*, which was defended in April 2008 at the University of Lisbon by Helena Ribeiro de Castro,[32] as well as from the fact that a new collective study on Mexican women teachers in the 19th and 20th centuries does not focus exclusively on lay women teachers, but also includes several contributions on teaching orders.[33] Finally, we can refer to a conference on the contribution of male and female religious to secondary education in Europe in the 19th and 20th centuries which took place in the Dutch city of Ravenstein in February 2009 and which was hosted by the 'European Forum on the History of Religious Institutes in the 19th and 20th Centuries' (RELINS-Europe).[34]

Of course, in some countries the topic has been studied more intensively than in others. Canada seems to be a real pioneer. To a considerable degree this is due to research by Elizabeth Smyth,[35] but many other Canadian scholars have published important studies on the subject and the diversity of topics and approaches is certainly remarkable.

Another notable fact is the complete absence of studies on women religious educators in two important long-running journals in the field of the history of education: the French *Histoire de l'Éducation* and the Spanish *Historia de la Educación*. Although it is rash to draw far-reaching conclusions from this, the complete ignoring of the subject in such important scholarly organs may not be entirely fortuitous. As long ago as 1998, Patrick Harrigan observed that Claude Langlois's important study "has not provoked in France the research into these schools [i.e. those run by women religious] that one might expect".[36] The neglect of the topic is certainly somewhat unexpected since both France and Spain have a strong Catholic tradition and are the homeland of many congregations.

Elements of a new historiography

In order to advance the study of both women religious educators and the schools run by them, as well as to renew the historiography of these subjects, several scholars have advocated following new approaches, using novel sources and applying new methodologies.

Noticing that "the field has, for too long, been dominated by works portraying Catholic education as divinely inspired altruism", Tom O'Donoghue and Anthony Potts asked that the religious teaching orders and the education which they provided be studied from a more secular perspective with ample attention being paid to the complex interaction of political, social, and economic forces.[37] They also stressed that researchers had to take into account the different categories of religious personnel. Finally, they argued that, over and above the traditional written sources, use should also be made of visual sources such as photographs, films and school architecture.

Stephanie Burley compared the approaches followed in a recent monograph on a South Australian Catholic girls' school headed by the Mercy Sisters with the newest insights concerning the historical study of the everyday educational reality (the so-called 'classroom history') and the use of visual and material sources. She concluded that the study of different types of sources is the best way to improve our understanding of social, cultural and pedagogical cultures in classrooms.[38]

Deirdre Raftery and Catherine Kilbride illustrated how visual images and oral recordings of Irish religious teachers can provide information on their work.[39] They also discussed the utilization of new technologies to record and archive the images and voices of those teachers. Elizabeth Smyth emphasized that it is extremely urgent that women religious be interviewed: "[f]or historians interested in oral history, women religious represent a declining resource. … Unless the stories and experience of these women religious are documented now, the details of their lives and work, as told in their own voices, will be lost forever".[40]

Inspired by the work of the Dutch theologian Annelies van Heijst, Marjet Derks recently warned against writing history from the sole perspective of the providers of education, i.e. the women religious.[41] She argued that we also need to take into account the experiences and practices of the receivers or 'consumers' of education, i.e. pupils, as well as the interactions between both groups. Since the receiver's perspective is "not neatly ordered in well-kept archives", this necessitates the development of new research methods. In a similar vein, Christine Lei pointed out that scholars have to seek out former students and/or their families in the search for yearbooks, photographs, letters, and other historical sources because the information obtained in this way can supplement the data derived from more official documents in diocesan and congregational archives.[42] Ultimately, it will widen our perspective on the lives of women religious, their students and their schools.

The oral-history-based research of Lies Van Rompaey on the marriage ban on Catholic women teachers in Belgium between 1920 and 1960 exposed the fact that women religious school administrators sometimes made new lay teachers sign a blank contract which was later filled in as a 'voluntary resignation' when the teacher married.[43] Her findings clearly demonstrate that lay women who taught in schools run by a congregation can provide useful information on women religious and the practices in their schools. Together with the statements of students, the evidence derived from such interviews can perhaps provide a counterbalance to the tendency to present the religious in an exclusively favourable light.

Rebecca Rogers made several important suggestions to renew the historiography of teaching congregations in 19th century France. She made a plea to position women religious as actors in the story of institutional development.[44] Having observed that the 'diaspora' of French religious teaching orders caused by the secularization offensive of the Third Republic has mainly been studied from the perspective of religious or missionary history and that the transmission of cultural values by French women teachers abroad has been largely ignored, she also advocated a more global, 'transnational' approach and she asked historians of education to be more attentive to issues of cultural interaction. Finally, she warned scholars not to be led astray by 19th century Catholic and anticlerical discourses and she urged them to undertake more nuanced analyses of the role of the teaching orders in girls' education because the subject has been approached in a caricatural way for far too long.[45] She said: "Il est temps d'en terminer avec l'image d'un catholicisme rétrograde et antiféministe. Le couvent des dames anglaises si bien décrit par Georges Sand n'est pas forcément caractéristique de toute l'éducation offerte par les religieuses".[46]

CHAPTER 3

Overview and assessment of the literature

Contribution to schooling

Women religious played a fundamental role in the schooling of girls of both the masses and the elite during the 19th and 20th centuries. In a study of the first decade of the Society of the Sacred Heart in St. Louis (1827-late 1830s), Nikola Baumgarten declared the teaching orders to be 'the pioneers of truly universal schooling', offering education open to girls and young women of all social, ethnic, cultural and religious backgrounds.[47] According to her, the fact that the Sacred Heart sisters provided the only educational opportunities for black, orphaned, and poor girls in St. Louis for nearly a decade shows that the Catholic teaching orders realized the principle of universal education long before the public schools.

Micheline Dumont described the contribution of women religious to schooling in Quebec as follows: "Elles ont conçu et organisé l'instruction secondaire et supérieure pour les filles; elles ont développé l'enseignement de la musique; elles ont organisé progressivement les principaux programmes de formation professionnelle spécifiquement destinés aux filles: école normale, écoles d'infirmières, écoles de secrétariat ou de métiers féminins, écoles professionnelles de musique; elles ont instauré et organisé l'enseignement ménager, le systématisant jusqu'à la création de deux facultés universitaires; elles ont inauguré et développé l'enseignement destiné aux clientèles dites exceptionnelles (délinquance, surdité, cécité, défience mentale, etc.); elles ont réussi à maintenir, pour les filles, des programmes d'études identiques à ceux des garçons, contre la volonté des principales autorités éducatives. Au bout du compte, force est de reconnaître que les religeuses ont été les principales responsables du développement des avenues éducatives pour les filles au Québec ...".[48] This list gives a clear indication of the immense extent of the educational work of Catholic women religious, but we are still very far removed from a complete mapping of the precise role which they played, both quantitatively and qualitatively, in the different educational domains in the various countries throughout the 19th and 20th centuries. Apart from a valuable article by Claude Langlois in which a modest effort was made to assess the immense contribution of the female congregations to education in 19th century France,[49] most studies merely give a panoramic overview of the wide spectrum of educational activities of the female teaching orders in a particular city,[50] region[51], country,[52] or language area.[53]

Some attention, however, has been paid to the role played by women religious in particular areas of education. According to Raymond Grew and Patrick Harrigan, the educational work of women religious possibly accelerated the spread of kindergartens in 19th century France.[54] When the teaching nun became a familiar figure, parents were more readily inclined to consign their pre-school children to pious care. In his excellent study on the rise and development of institutions for early childhood education in France, Jean-Noël Luc showed that the female religious orders played a fundamental part in establishing and staffing the so-called *salles d'asile*, i.e. institutions which were intended to care for and to educate the very young children of the rural and urban poor while their parents worked.[55] Whereas this kind of charitable enterprise originated in a lay and often Protestant milieu during the July Monarchy (1830-1848) the involvement of the orders grew substantially, and at the end of the 1870s, on the eve of the creation of a national system of *écoles maternelles* by the republican government, about 75% of the *salles d'asile* were run by Catholic women religious. More than ten years ago Luc noticed that more research was needed on the contribution of individual congregations to early childhood education, and even today case studies of congregations involved in the care of pre-school children are still extremely rare.[56]

Several scholars have reassessed the contribution of women religious to primary education in France. In a broad quantitative study on the growth of elementary education from 1821 to 1906, Raymond Grew and Patrick Harrigan demonstrated that universal primary education was achieved largely through the male and female teaching orders.[57] The educational legislation issued by the republican authorities in the early 1880s (the 'Ferry Laws') did not create a system of primary schooling out of nothing; it merely regularized, secularized, and improved it. Through the provision of education in one of the areas in which the public system was extremely weak, i.e. the schooling of girls, the female teaching orders played a very considerable role in the development of universal primary education. Sarah Curtis made an in-depth case study of the situation in the diocese of Lyons to evaluate the contribution of male and female teaching orders to universal primary education in 19th century France.[58] According to her, the congregations became important providers of education as a result of several factors: the high local demands for primary schooling, the failure of the French state to provide the finance to meet these demands, the eagerness of the Catholic Church to monopolize primary education, the availability of huge numbers of brothers and sisters, and the active support of local elites.

The important role of the female teaching congregations in the emergence of the secondary school system for girls in 19th century France was highlighted in the new research by Rebecca Rogers.[59] Contrary to the traditional view, based on an uncritical reading of republican-biased sources, the new national system of secondary education for girls was not founded out of the blue in 1880 by the law of Camille Sée, but it was built upon a network of existing private schools staffed by nuns and lay women teachers.

Bernd Zymek and Gabriele Neghabian debunked another persistent myth. The quantitative data which they collected about the secondary schools for girls in Germany from 1800 to 1945 contradict the widely held view that the *Kulturkampf* legislation marked the end of the growth of schools operated by orders of women religious in Prussia.[60] In the 1890s, after the moderation and repeal of the secularization laws, a new wave of school foundations started in Prussia and Bavaria which continued until World War I. This finding confirms the conclusions arrived at earlier by Relinde Meiwes in her general study of women congregations in 19th century Prussia[61] and it illustrates the fundamental role played by sisters in the provision of secondary education in particular regions of Germany.

Mary Oates assessed the importance of the convent academies in the US.[62] She showed that by founding scores of such academies in the 19th century – in 1820 there were ten such schools, by 1860 they numbered 202 – the female communities made an important contribution to women's educational progress in the period before public secondary schools developed. Their quick response to the growing demand for girls' education beyond the primary level made them pioneers, especially in many western states of the US. When free public high schools spread in late 19th century, Protestant enrollment strongly declined, but this was compensated for by the increase in children from the rapidly growing Catholic middle and upper classes. In this way the academies contributed to the integration of 19th century Catholics into mainstream American society. No less important, they set the stage for the development of Catholic colleges for women in the 20th century.

Besides attempts to explore the contribution of individual congregations to the higher education sector,[63] scholars in North America and Ireland have started to map the general involvement of religious communities in the provision of post-secondary education for women.[64] Their research shows that the Catholic hierarchy was originally reluctant to support the movement for the higher education of women and altered its position only as a result of the perceived threat posed by the emerging Protestant and state institutions. Some scholars have emphasized that the women religious played a crucial role in convincing the hierarchy to found colleges for Catholic women, and even used the card of denominational rivalry strategically.[65] Once the Church authorities had given them the green light, the teaching orders became key players in women's higher education. Judith Harford pointed out that by the beginning of the 20th century the Catholic women's colleges in Ireland had surpassed their Protestant counterparts,[66] and Thomas Landy showed that by the 1950s the Catholic women's colleges established by congregations of women religious in the US educated a slightly larger cohort of women than did Protestant or non-denominational institutions.[67] In the US the exponential growth of these institutions came to a halt only in the late 1950s, and after 1968 the number of colleges dropped sharply.

In many countries nuns have also provided more specialized education, such as training in teaching, nursing, domestic science, agriculture, music, administration and secretaryship. According to Micheline Dumont, women religious in Quebec were controlling almost completely the vocational training of girls in 1960; only a few so-called feminine professions – library science, social services and dietetics – had developed outside their influence.[68]

Specialized studies of the huge contribution of women religious to the training of teachers are rare,[69] but the involvement of congregations is discussed in some general histories of teacher training.[70] With regard to Quebec Marie-Paule Malouin and Thérèse Hamel drew attention to the fact that in the middle of the 19th century the State and the Church had in a way divided the task of training future teachers: the State supervised the training of male student teachers, while the training of females was the responsibility of nuns.[71] This division was preserved even after the State-Church dispute on the control of Normal Schools in Quebec in the late 19th century.[72] Mineke van Essen pointed out that the teacher training centre created by the *Tilburgse Zusters van Liefde* in their mother house in 1852 (the so-called '*educandaat*') was the first teacher training school for women in the Netherlands.[73]

Despite the huge role played by the sisters in the schooling of nurses, standard histories on nursing training have generally not addressed the contribution of Catholic sisters.[74] Likewise, the domestic science education and the specialized music training provided by the women religious have not been the subject of systematic studies.[75]

Historians of education have started to examine the involvement of sisters in what now is termed 'special education', but beyond case studies of the educational work undertaken by individual congregations for children in need, such as physically disabled or mentally retarded children,[76] orphans or abandoned children,[77] and 'wayward' or delinquent young women,[78] the subject remains relatively underexplored.[79]

Even though female congregations were in the first place involved in the education of girls, they sometimes also taught boys and even adults. These aspects of the educational contribution of women religious have received scant attention so far and need to be canvassed more fully.

A very particular and little-known dimension of the involvement of women religious in childcare and education is the role they played in rescuing Jewish children from the Nazis. Suzanne Vromen recently described this forgotten episode in a wonderful book on the Belgian nuns who risked their lives by sheltering children in their convents.[80]

Since most teaching sisters were active in private schools, the schooling they offered provided in many cases an important alternative for groups of people excluded and/or culturally oppressed by the dominant system, such as Catholics in certain regions or countries, as well as language minorities. Isabelle Bourgeois, for example, described how a school in Ottawa run by the Congregation of the Grey Nuns of the Cross (later the Sisters of Charity) enabled French-speaking girls to study in their first language, something which was impossible in the public schools.[81]

Several scholars have drawn attention to the fact that Catholic sisters also taught in public schools. Florence Deacon has pointed to their work in the public district schools in frontier Wisconsin.[82] Deirdre Raftery and Catherine Nowlan-Roebuck have analysed how the Presentation Order managed to work within the new secular education system in 19th century Ireland.[83] With regard to Quebec in the 19th century, Canadian scholars have established that the income which the sisters derived from tuition and boarding in their private schools allowed them to teach in public schools, and that the public school system was thus indirectly subsidized by the private system.[84] The renowned feminist Germaine Greer, who was herself educated by nuns, expressed her opinion that "the Australian education system would have collapsed without the exploitation of this group of women".[85] What is clear is that a lot more research is still needed to provide a precise idea of the extent of the involvement of the teaching orders in the public educational system.

Teaching orders and schools

The vast majority of the publications about the involvement of women religious in education are histories either of individual teaching orders or of individual educational establishments conducted by them. Many are book-length monographs, but some are just articles.

A limited number of congregation histories deal specifically with the educational work of the order, such as for example the impressive monograph on the *Zusters der Christelijke Scholen van Vorselaar* by Raf Vanderstraeten and Marij Preneel, and Maire Kealy's recent study of the role of Dominican women in Irish education.[86]

Most congregation histories are of a more general nature, and usually include only shorter discussions on the order's involvement in teaching.[87] As historians of education, we do of course regret it when a study pays more attention to the spiritual and communal life of the women than to their role as educators,[88] but we do subscribe to the viewpoint of Jean de Viguerie: "Les instituts religieux enseignants méritent d'être étudiés pour eux-mêmes, en eux-mêmes, et non seulement dans leur activité d'enseignement. Comment comprendre une pédagogie sans remonter à sa source, l'esprit de la congrégation, sa finalité propre?"[89]

A large number of publications about teaching orders, especially articles, focus on specific events in the history of a congregation, such as its foundation and early history,[90] conflicts with the church authorities,[91] opposition from Protestants,[92] difficulties caused by the wave of secularization in the late 19th and early 20th centuries (e.g. the laicization laws of the French Third Republic,[93] the *Kulturkampf* in Germany and Switzerland[94] and the 'school confict' in the Netherlands[95]) or the troubled period under the National Socialist regime in Germany.[96]

School histories that contain the life story of a single educational institution largely staffed and/or run by a religious community are a related category of publications.[97] Sometimes special attention is paid to a particular period in the history of the school such as the founding years,[98] the period during which the school had to face particularly strong anti-Catholic opposition,[99] or the years in which the school opened its doors to black pupils (*i.c.* African Americans).[100]

Whereas numerous histories of religious congregations were written by a member of the community, many school histories are the work of someone who has studied or worked (or both) within the school described, and both kinds of histories are usually published on the occasion of a jubilee.

School jubilee volumes and congregation histories have long been of questionable quality. Based on an analysis of a number of school jubilee volumes published in Belgium between 1977 and 1982, Frank Simon concluded that these works give historians little reason to be jubilant.[101] Many works are inward looking, anecdotal and sometimes even hagiographic and triumphalist. Often they make no serious use of sources and scholarly literature, lack a critical approach, and pay insufficient attention to the broader social, economic, political and religious context. The same applies to the more amateurish congregation histories written by insiders. Marie-Paule Malouin noted: "Reconstituer l'histoire de sa congrégation lorsqu'on est religieuse constitue sans doute un défi de taille. C'est un peu écrire l'histoire de sa propre famille. Il doit être difficile de garder une certaine distance entre l'auteur et son objet d'études, de ne pas s'identifier à cet objet de l'analyse".[102]

Fortunately, things have changed for the better. As Paul Wynants, the author of an important methodological article on historical research on schools conducted by a congregation,[103] observed in 2002, the newer memorial books usually do not display the flaws which characterized them in the past.[104] In many instances, congregations or schools have asked one or more professional historians to write a history of their community or establishment. Moreover, the works written by sisters are generally also of a higher quality than they used to be. Despite the undeniable progress, Wynants noted that they are not entirely satisfactory because they focus strictly on the internal history of the institution and discuss almost exclusively institutional aspects. Though this cannot be denied, it is hardly surprising since the works are of course first and foremost intended as histories of institutions.

Guy Laperrière asked himself whether it is useful to write a history of every congregation of some importance.[105] He observed that in almost every history the same scheme appears: an impressive foundress, difficult beginnings, a period of expansion from the mid-19th century until about 1965 (usually in the domain of education), considerable upheaval starting with Vatican Council II in the 1960s, a renovation process around 1968-1969, the exodus of sisters and a declining number of entries, the progressive abandoning of traditional apostolic works, new commitments, ageing, and, finally, hope for the future. On the other hand, he pointed out that every congregation has its own characteristics, charism, and spirituality, operates in its own milieu, and has its own influence. In his opinion, these particular aspects make the writing of histories of religious communities a useful undertaking.

On the question "How does one write a history of a religious community?", Laperrière gave the following answer: "Il faut d'abord une problématique, une ligne de fond, qui réponde aux questions que se posent nos contemporains ou, au moins, que se pose l'auteur. Une passion qui constitue le fil conducteur. Ensuite, il est fort utile de fournir les données de base …".[106] Unfortunately, most histories are not based upon a research question or do not take a specific angle as their point of departure. Reviewing several congregation histories, Laperrière also noticed one other recurring weakness: the lack of analysis. Most histories indeed present the facts without actually discussing or analysing them; they usually do not venture into interpretation any further than is factually evident.

Most studies are instances of what might be called 'descriptive micro-history'. They provide 'objective' documentation on a narrow, well-defined subject. They can be regarded as well-developed case studies, but, being limited in scope, they rarely provide the material necessary to determine whether the subject studied is typical or rather peculiar.

This characterization is in no way intended to belittle the importance of these works. As Antonio Viñao observed, trying to prove the primacy of either descriptive micro-history or more interpretative macro-history is rather pointless.[107] Generalization and particularization are "two inseparable processes: the two sides of a coin, neither of which can do without the other".

Congregation and school histories are not works in which one will find broad working hypotheses, and they do not directly add to more general debates; but, on the other hand, they provide fundamental building materials for macro-history, including an abundance of chronological, biographical and quantitative data, as well as rich visual documentation. One might say that they form the link between raw, unexploited archival sources and broad generalizing histories.

The historian who wishes to write a broad synthesis is confronted by a huge number of such histories and, since they have often been privately printed or published by small, local publishing houses, they are not generally available in libraries. Maybe a large-scale book digitization programme could bring these widely dispersed sources together?

Whereas more in-depth case studies are still needed, we would like to urge scholars to write national or regional syntheses on the basis of the histories which have appeared on schools and congregations in their own countries or regions. Only in this way can the richness of these studies gradually be used to develop broader theories and hypotheses.

It is far beyond the scope of this contribution to give a detailed overview of congregation and school histories, but we would like to mention a few innovative and important examples.

Examining the foundation of the Missionary Oblate Sisters of the Sacred Heart and Mary Immaculate in Manitoba (Canada), Rosa Bruno-Jofre discovered that the sisters had developed their own interpretation of the foundation and the roles played by different people.[108] Her study can be categorized as a critical search for the real foundation history of the order, as well as an exploration of what William McNeill called 'mythistory', i.e. "what groups of people have known and believed about their past and found necessary to preserve as essential for their existence".[109]

Elizabeth Smyth and Linda Wicks undertook an oral history project in order to capture the history of the teaching congregation of the Sisters of St. Joseph of Toronto in the words of its members.[110]

The article which Christine Lei published on the Loretto School for Girls in Hamilton (Province of Ontario in Canada) is remarkable because of its focus on the location of the school, the architecture of the school buildings, as well as the artefacts and imagery inside and outside the complex.[111]

With *Growing Good Catholic Girls*, a reworked version of a PhD thesis presented at the University of Sydney, Christine Trimingham Jack has produced what may be called a model of a 'postmodern school history'.[112] Her well-researched account of Kerever Park, a preparatory convent boarding school for middle class girls located in the Southern Highlands in Australia (to the south west of Sydney) during the years 1944 to 1965, is based on a variety of sources, including fourteen oral interviews with ex-students, sisters of the French Society of the Sacred Heart who ran the school and one married couple employed by the sisters. Being a former student of the school, the author has also incorporated her own experiences and perceptions. Strong and original features are the analysis of visual materials such as the symbols of the congregation as they appear in a painting in the school vestibule, the study of the influence of architecture and landscape, and attention to the marginalized group of 'lay sisters'.[113] The author has also described the psychological effects which Vatican Council II had on some of the teaching sisters. Trimmingham Jack has published separate articles on particular topics in relation to the school, and these will be discussed further in the section on educational philosophy.

Marie-Paule Malouin's monograph on a girls' school of the *Soeurs des Saints Noms de Jésus et de Marie* in a Montreal parish from 1876 tot 1911 is less innovative as regards its methodology – it is a sound historical study based on written archival records – but it is particularly interesting because it is a school history as well as a case study of the relationship between private and public schools in Quebec in the late 19th and early 20th centuries.[114] The sisters taught in two schools which were originally both located in one building: the private school *l'Académie Marie-Rose*, a boarding school for the children of well-to-do parents who could afford to pay tuition and boarding fees, and the public school *l'École paroissale de Saint-Jean-Baptiste*, an establishment offering free education to day students from poor families. Malouin demonstrated that, in comparison with the pupils of the academy, the children of the public school were discriminated against in many ways. The parish school took in 75% of the pupils and the classes were much bigger. The classrooms were smaller and less well-equipped with furniture and teaching materials. The public school offered no educational services like a library, the celebrations and prize-giving ceremonies were much more modest, and the children had no opportunity to continue their studies for as long as the students in the private school. Malouin concluded that the income from education and boarding fees paid by the parents of the children in the academy formed the financial backbone of the sisters and enabled them to provide education to children from the lower classes with only minimal financial support from the local school committee. Or, as she formulated it: "l'école privée 'subventionne' l'école publique en cette fin du XIXe siècle".[115]

Finally, we would like to draw attention to an original study produced by a team of scholars about a South Australian Catholic girls' school administered by the Mercy Sisters.[116] Instead of the study following a chronological approach, the different parts of the school are analysed one after the other: classroom, staffroom, chapel, playground, etc.

Educational philosophy, content and practice

Regarding the situation in mid-19th century France, Rebecca Rogers observed that the general features of the mission of the teaching congregations was the same: '[r]eligious teachers sought to form good Christian women whose influence would then spread throughout society through their daily actions within the family and through charitable actions in society as a whole'.[117] On the other hand, she noticed that the characteristics of their mission evolved over time and that there were significant nuances according to the stature of the order and the social milieu targeted.[118]

Historians of American Catholic education have arrived at similar conclusions. In her work on the rise and growth of Catholic education in Detroit, JoEllen McNergney Vinyard remarked that the three communities of sisters who staffed the overwhelming majority of Detroit schools had a common Catholic educational mission, but a widely different educational philosophy.[119] On the basis of his analysis of the emergence of Catholic education in Chicago and Milwaukee Timothy Walch concluded that before the 1930s there was more uniformity in the textbooks, curriculum, and teaching methods among the schools of one religious order spread across the country than among the schools of different parishes in Chicago.[120]

These findings strongly suggest that, at least with regard to the period before a more unified system of Catholic education came into being, the educational philosophy, content and practice of each teaching congregation has to be studied separately before generalizations and comparisons can be made. This is a huge task which has barely begun.

When Charles Molette drew up the balance of the research presented at the French conference on the history of female teaching orders in 1980, he noted that more research was needed to determine the influence of the spirituality of the congregations on the education they provided.[121] Twenty-nine years later the complicated issue of the relationship between the order's charisma on the one hand and the educational philosophy, content and practice on the other has still hardly been addressed.

Educational philosophy

Precisely to fill this lacuna, Lorna Bowman attempted to provide an interpretive framework to clarify the relationship between the influence of the founding vision of a religious congregation and the educational philosophy it developed.[122] The methodological approach she proposed is based on the observation that in Max Weber's study of the phenomenon of charisma in institution building it is assumed that there was no 'deep chasm' between the charismatic aspects (i.e. the charismatic quality of the leader, *in casu* the founder of the congregation) and the more ordinary, routine aspects of social organization and the life of social institutions (*in casu* the religious congregation). In the process of routinization, the founder's charisma is transformed into stable forms of thought, practice and organization. Lorman concluded that, using a primarily sociological conceptualization for interpretation, it is possible to ascertain the influence of the charismatic founder of a religious congregation on the educational philosophy of a teaching congregation.

The primary sources in the study of the broader educational mission of the congregation and its specific ideas regarding pedagogics and didactics are written documents such as congregation constitutions, teaching manuals, internally produced textbooks, promotional material and school newspapers. An approach focusing on written sources was followed by, for example, Lorna Bowman and Roseanne McDougall in their studies on the educational philosophy of Cornelia Connelly, the founder of the Society of the Holy Child Jesus in England.[123]

However, as Christine Trimingham Jack showed in her book on a school run by the Society of the Sacred Heart in Australia from 1944 to 1965, oral evidence as well as visual and material sources such as the architecture, furnishings, location and surroundings of a school, can also provide useful information on the educational intentions of a congregation.

In a separate contribution Trimingham Jack exposed the competing educational discourses in the history of the school.[124] Built as a country-house, the school was originally intended as a home where children could have a happy and innocent childhood. Soon, however, the school became an instrument for moulding children into obedient members of the Church and society and to prepare them for the afterlife. Following a theory of Colin Symes that the 'symbolic climate' of a school is enshrined in the school vestibule and the artefacts displayed there,[125] she demonstrated that the painting of Saint Madeleine Sophie, the foundress of the order and a canonized saint, which decorated the hall visualized all the key pedagogic discourses of the school: education in the service of God (the Sacred

Heart statue oversees all), education oriented to the traditional role of women (the children's attention is drawn to a painting of Mary the mother of Jesus, the so-called '*Mater Admirabilis* icon'), pursuit of perfection (the pink ribbon which one child is wearing as a sign of merit), and intellectual rigour (the books tucked under the children's arms).

In another article Trimingham Jack discussed in more detail the significance of the three sacred symbols of the Society of the Sacred Heart which appear together in the painting in the hall, i.e. the Sacred Heart (a symbol of Jesus), Saint Madeleine Sophie and *Mater Admirabilis*. She showed convincingly that they were the bearers of powerful educational discourses.[126] In a third paper she examined in what way the location of the school, its architectural style and the nature of its garden may throw light on the educational aims of the congregation.[127]

Trimingham Jack's work strongly reflects the belief that the architecture, environment and material culture of a school can be analysed as records of educational intentions, and contains several useful elements of such an analysis, but a rigorous and systematic 'reading' of the school building, its furnishings and its surroundings according to the newest insights of architectural/spatial analysis and the study of the materialities of schooling still has to be undertaken for a school run by sisters.[128] Such an in-depth investigation into one school or a group of schools would probably be most rewarding since the elaborate building complexes of convent schools seem very suitable subjects for this kind of analysis.[129]

Researchers should not only pay attention to the 'official' educational philosophy of teaching congregations and to the various media through which this was proclaimed – either overtly or less overtly – they should also try to uncover the more 'hidden' aspects of the motivations and intentions of the congregations. One possible new line of enquiry might be to focus on the impact of 'market mechanisms' on the educational ideology of the various teaching congregations, i.e. the rivalry with other educational providers – public as well as private – in the struggle to occupy a niche in the 'education market'.[130] It might be interesting to investigate whether the specific identity of a teaching congregation was primarily derived from the spirituality of the community as it was established at the time of its foundation or whether it was 'forged' in the course of time out of a more prosaic concern to achieve a secure place in the educational landscape.

Finally, it is essential that the educational intentions of teaching sisters are not studied merely for their own sake, but that they are compared with the outcome of their educational activities. In a case study of the education provided by the

Soeurs des Saints Noms de Jésus et de Marie in a Montreal parish in the 19th century, Marie-Paule Malouin made an important observation in this regard: "Malgré le conformisme des objectifs visés dans l'éducation des filles, les religieuses enseignantes vont déclencher un mécanisme évolutif dont pour la plupart, elles ne sont probablement pas conscientes".[131] Whereas the education given to the girls was aimed not at orienting them towards a professional career, but at preparing them for their future roles as wives and mothers, the very fact that the girls received a sound education meant that some of them as adults questioned the traditional values and chose a different role in society. A similar observation was made by Francis O'Hagan in his study of the contribution of the congregations to education in Glasgow: "[u]ndoubtedly, the promotion of marriage and family life to these young women remained centrally important but the orders also gave their female pupils many of the tools that their daughters and granddaughters would use to challenge the subordination of women in the subsequent decades".[132]

Educational content

Since the educational content in a sense forms the *trait d'union* around which the pedagogical and didactic relationship between the teacher and the pupil is constructed,[133] it is impossible to imagine a modern history of education without 'curriculum history'.[134]

A modest start has been made in analysing the curricular materials used by the teaching congregations and, again, Canadian researchers have taken the lead. We can refer to the research done by Andrée Dufour on a series of textbooks on sciences which were produced by the *Soeurs de Sainte-Anne* between 1923 and 1956.[135] Among other things, she has tried to find out which topics were given preeminence and what the difference was between the science curriculum for girls and boys. Monique Lebrun has investigated the conception of literature in French textbooks which were published by Quebec communities of both male and female religious in the first half of the 20th century.[136] In her impressive bibliography of Canadian cookery books, Elizabeth Driver not only gave full bibliographical descriptions of the textbooks produced for cookery classes by the teaching congregations in Quebec; she also made a general observation on the contents of these books: the opening discourse on the moral dimensions of cookery and the scope for practising virtue in the kitchen which appears in the very first recipe manual by a member of a religious order (*Directions diverses données par la rev. mère Caron ... pour aider ses sœurs à former de bonnes cuisinières*, Montreal, 1878) became a typical feature of textbooks produced by the '*écoles ménagères*' of the teaching orders in Quebec in the 20th century.[137]

Some historians have covered the differences between the curriculum of girls' secondary schools directed by women religious and the teaching programme in public high schools. According to Micheline Dumont, the inclusion of music in the curriculum was 'the only authentic innovation' in convent schools in 19th century Quebec.[138] In a case study of St. Ann's Academy in British Columbia (Canada), a school run by the Sisters of St. Ann, Meg Stanley pointed out that, especially through the 1950s, the availability of specialized instruction in art, music, and, to a lesser degree, commercial studies was what set St. Ann's apart from public high schools.[139] She also observed that, after the adoption of the provincial programme of studies, the curriculum at St. Ann's was distinguished mainly by the addition of instruction in religion and weekly lessons in etiquette and morals. As scholars usually tend to focus either on private secondary schools administered by nuns or on public high schools,[140] systematic comparisons of the curriculum in both types of schools have not so far been undertaken.

A topic which has received a lot of attention is the nature of the curriculum in girls' secondary schools run by women religious. Two conflicting visions emerge from the literature. One group of scholars subscribes to the traditional view that the education offered by the sisters is rather narrow and conservative. In her study of eleven academies in the American Midwest between 1860 and 1920, Eileen Brewer stressed that refinement and religion formed the core of the education provided.[141] She observed that "the education provided by such academies had far more to do with inculcating good breeding and Catholic culture in young women than with preparing them for college, marriage, or the workplace", and she noted that this was "in marked contrast to the efforts of comparable Protestant institutions founded by educational reformers".

Anne Gagnon argued that the education which the girls received in a boarding school in the province of Alberta in Canada between 1926 and 1960 was in the first place intended to transform them into competent housewives, good companions to their husbands, and able educators of their children.[142] With that aim, they received solid training in the domestic sciences and they were taught the 'qualities of the heart', such as the value of affection, tenderness and the ability to console and to understand. The Virgin Mary was presented as the model which they had to emulate.

On the basis of a study of a French private school for the girls of well-to-do families run by the *Congrégation de Notre-Dame*, Monique de Saint Martin arrived at the conclusion that even in the second half of the 20th century one of the most important aims of this type of establishment was to reproduce the traditional sexual division of labour and power in the family.[143] Young girls of the bourgeoisie and aristocracy were prepared to become the mothers of 'happy families', cultivated, discrete and efficacious wives ready to assist their husbands in their professional activity, devoted women eager to offer their cooperation to new charitable works and mistresses of the house carefully administering the social and symbolic capital of the family.

In her paper on two South Australian Catholic girls' schools in the 1920s, Stephanie Burley noticed that religion underpinned the entire curriculum,[144] and so did Marjet Derks in her study on a secondary school of the Ursulines in Nijmegen in the first half of the 20th century.[145] Although the latter labelled the education offered by the sisters as 'broad', she stressed that in the first place the students learned to become Catholic women. She pointed out: "Their talents had to be developed, but they were not meant to be too outstanding as individuals. The emphasis was more on becoming part of an outstanding group and community".[146]

Other scholars have challenged the rather negative image of the education provided in the schools of the religious orders. Generally, they did this on three grounds. First, two Canadian scholars observed that the uniformly negative image can no longer be held when one fully takes into consideration the temporal and geographical dimension. Elizabeth Smyth disputed that in the 19th and early 20th centuries all Catholic convent academies in English Canada were places "focusing mainly on moral education, social graces and solicitation of new members for the order", instead stressing that there was an important evolution in the curriculum of such schools.[147] She showed that the school run by the Sisters of St. Joseph in Toronto moved from a curriculum "which emphasized moral and polite deportment" to "one which qualified them [the students] for teaching, post-secondary education and entrance to the world of work". She also observed that by 1882 the sisters had adapted their curriculum to comply with provincial standards. Finally, she cited convincing quantitative evidence which nuances the widely held – but usually unsubstantiated – view that operating a boarding school was primarily a means to attract new members for the order: of the 2,338 pupils listed between 1856 and 1920, only 104 girls (4.4%) entered the Toronto community as novices. Christine Lei noted that by 1889 the curriculum in the Loretto School for Girls in Hamilton, Ontario, had undergone considerable revision and had become more academically rigorous. She also drew attention to the fact that the education in a Loretto convent in Ireland differed greatly from Loretto convent education in Ontario.[148] Whereas the former offered a limited curriculum in harp playing, embroidery, and pottery, the latter taught both accomplishments and academic subjects. She also pointed out that some of the convent schools in Hamilton offered science courses as early as in

1865, whereas at the time science was entirely absent from the curriculum of the public high school in Hamilton.

Secondly, Lorna Bowman pointed out that the negative image of the education offered by women religious might be the result of interpreting the school curriculum on the basis of anachronistic or biased conceptions.[149] Following Marjorie Theobald's observation that the historic assessment of female education "has fallen victim to male/bureaucratic definitions of education and professionalism" and subscribing to her call "to reinterpret its language, symbols and forms" and "to reconsider its importance to women as teachers and pupils",[150] Bowman explained that education which included the accomplishments is not a priori inferior, role-reinforcing or conservative. She admitted that the education provided by the Society of the Holy Child Jesus in schools in England during the 19th century was in line with the strictures of society and socialized the girls, but she argued that it did more than that: it was built on the accomplishments tradition in a manner which was liberating for the young women as they were taught to be self-reliant.

Thirdly, many have argued that the negative image surrounding the education provided by teaching sisters is the result of a biased, i.e. anti-Catholic or androcentric rhetoric. According to Maurits De Vroede, the uniformly static and negative image of Catholic boarding schools for girls in Belgium before World War I, i.e. that the instruction and education offered in those institutions was qualitatively inferior and that the curriculum was entirely oriented towards formalism, has its origins in the anticlerical campaign during the 'school funding controversy' (1878-1884).[151] Although he admitted that the girls were educated with a bias towards piety and virtue, he stressed that the traditional view which states that these schools taught only the *arts d'agréments* can no longer be held, and he demonstrated that existing programmes were adapted as a result of changes in society.

The persistent view that in 19th century France the secondary schools conducted by nuns raised girls merely as 'superstitious ignoramuses' was traced by Rebecca Rogers back to the traditional 'republican' historiography which uncritically embraced the discourse of the anti-Catholic policy of the Third Republic: since women religious teachers lived in a world completely alien to the real world, the education they transmitted inevitably ran counter to modern values, and it was the state which saved girls from the arms of the church by establishing high-quality secondary education for girls![152] Rogers noted that the education provided in the *Légion d'honneur* schools headed by the *Congrégation de la Mère de Dieu* was actually more progressive than that in the Legion of Honour school directed by lay women. Whereas the secular women teachers' school tried to maintain traditional bourgeois representations of women's roles through a curriculum which remained resolutely non-professional, the congregational schools offered a programme which not only placed emphasis on intellectual education, but also prepared their students for an active future through the learning of vocational or professional skills. Although she admits that the schools examined by her are not necessarily representative of all schools administered by sisters, she stresses that these findings strongly suggest that the religious teaching orders were sensitive to the new professional opportunities available to women and showed a great willingness to adapt their curricula to the changing socio-economic circumstances. As Rogers pointed out, the new public secondary schools for women created by the Republican government were even more retrograde than the schools of the teaching congregations because they were exclusively oriented towards domestic matters.

In Anna Barbaro's opinion, the thesis that prior to 1920 the primary aim of secondary education for Catholic girls in Australia was "domestic, moral, religious and accomplishment attainment", with only "some interest in academic achievement", was falsely put forward by parish priests and bishops who usually acted as spokesmen for women religious.[153] She argued that after 1870 the convent schools for girls in Australia placed greater emphasis on the academic curriculum and that the education provided by them included practically all the elements usually associated with boys' education, such as Geometry, Algebra and Latin. Drawing attention to the fact that the girls' education which the religious teaching orders had brought to Australia in the 19th century was based on the Jesuit model, she reclaimed an unbroken academic tradition for women's education.

Observing that the explosive growth of Catholic academies for girls in the U.S. during the 19th century gave rise to a strong anti-Catholic rhetoric because many Protestants feared that Catholicism would gain a hold on the new public in these schools, Carol Mattingly argued that it is precisely this rhetoric which is responsable for the misconception that the Catholic academies provided only a narrow curriculum completely dominated by religion.[154] In fact, the Catholic convent academies offered a rigorous education of academic quality and, as a result of the hostile rhetoric surrounding the Catholic academies and the willingness to attract pupils from Protestant families, these academies even placed less emphasis on religion than the Protestant academies, which gave religion a more central place in the curriculum in order to consolidate Protestantism amidst what they perceived as a form of Catholic threat.

In her study on American convent academies Mary Oates took a middle position in the debate.[155] Observing that in the 1820s French sisterhoods provided an education which included Latin and other subjects not typically part of a female curriculum, she rejected the critism by educational reformers like Catharine Beecher that convent academies overemphasized the value of feminine accomplishments to the detriment of more intellectual courses. However, regarding convent academies in the middle of the century, she considered the criticism well-founded: "[r]ather than joining in the educational reform movement well underway in Protestant academies by mid-century, convent schools instead persisted in offering curricula tailored to the limited expectations of upper-class parents".[156]

The transmission of cultural values through the curriculum is another important topic. It has mainly been addressed in studies on the education of the children of Catholic immigrants in America. These children received their education in parish schools which were usually run by male or female religious orders originating from the same country as the immigrants. In his study on the establishment and growth of Catholic schooling in Chicago and Milwaukee from its inception until the 1930s, Timothy Walch refuted the argument, put forward by critics of parochial education, that parish schools "have been fundamentally divisive because they preserved ethnic and religious traditions at the expense of American values".[157] His analysis of textbooks, albeit of a male teaching order (the Christian Brothers of Ireland), made him conclude that, apart from the greater emphasis on moral and religious issues, the education did not substantially differ from that given in public schools. The curriculum also stressed traditional values such as patriotism, diligence, and deference to authority.

William Galush studied the Americanization of the curriculum in the Polish-American parochial schools.[158] He found that, during the 1930s, nationalistic sentiment towards the old country had largely disappeared from the textbooks, whereas there was a stronger identification with core elements of American political culture. He also observed that there was subtle encouragement within the teaching congregation to use more non-Polish curricular materials. Although a sense of ethnicity remained, instruction moved from Polish to English and – as he put it – "Janek became Johnny".

Kim Tolley neatly summarized the debate about the impact of the ethnically and linguistically diverse parochial schools in the US as follows: "Those who viewed the extinction of cultural differences as an important component of Americanization construed the etnic parish school as divisive and politically dangerous. But those who viewed Americanization as a fusion of diverse cultural strands conceded the social benefit of the Catholic school, a place where the immigrant learned to successfully make the transition from old world to new".[159]

When, just before World War I, Reverend Edmund H. Oliver investigated the elementary schools in rural parts of the Canadian province of Saskatchewan, he concluded that the primary schools in the area settled by German Catholics posed a threat to the Canadianization of the province because the children were taught German and the teachers were unable to teach in English. Clinton White, however, convincingly showed that this picture of the elementary school situation is not only erroneous and incomplete, but also that Oliver intentionally belittled the education provided by the German Catholics.[160] In order to reinforce the Anglo-Celtic cultural hegemony in an area with an ethnically diverse population, he wished to promote a policy of 'English only' in all elementary schools. Clinton refuted Oliver's argument that the teachers were not fluent in English: though the Ursulines all came directly from Germany, some were British or American. He also pointed out that, except for one hour of instruction in German every day, the sisters taught only in English! Finally, he showed that shortly after the Ursuline Sisters began teaching at St. Peter Parochial School, they also taught Canadian patriotic songs. So, the least one can say is that Oliver's report can no longer be used as a reliable source to determine whether ethnic-based schools preserved cultural traditions at the expense of national values.

Evidently, the courses offered by schools, as reflected in their official prospectuses, and the textbooks say more about the intentions of the educators than what is actually taught by the teacher or what was actually 'absorbed' by the students. So, instead of focusing exclusively on what the educators believed the students should be taught (the 'formal curriculum'), it might also be useful to pay attention to the actual curriculum delivered and presented by each teacher (the 'curriculum-in-use'), as well as to what the students perceived they learnt.[161]

Another important subject is the 'hidden curriculum', i.e. "the kinds of learnings children derive from the very nature and organizational design of the school, as well as from the behaviors and attitudes of teachers and administrators".[162] In their study of American teaching sisterhoods and convent academy curricula Carol Coburn and Martha Smith observed that, unlike the formal curricula which were adapted over time in response to evolutions in society, the hidden curriculum remained amazingly constant.[163]

The way in which students were influenced by the behaviour, attitudes and values of sisters is difficult to detect and to analyse. Barbara Boggs Sigmund, a former student of several Sacred Heart schools and ex-Mayor of Princeton, New Jersey, testified that the sisters provided powerful role models for the pupils.[164] By demonstrating that they were perfectly able to run their institutions on their own, they instilled self-confidence and self-control in the girls. She even remembered having read "statistical evidence in the early 1980's indicating that disproportionate numbers of women in political and corporate office in the United States were graduates of Roman Catholic girls' schools". Stephanie Burley wondered to what extent women religious gave somewhat contradictory messages to their students by the very lives they were leading, "at times appearing powerful, independent and educated, yet at others enshrining the virtues of obedience, submission and virginity".[165] Rebecca Rogers also noted the contradiction between the piety, obedience, and submission they taught and the messages offered by their lives of responsible, powerful, dynamic and independent women.[166]

Christine Lei showed how the formal and hidden curricula could intersect in a science class of the Loretto Academy in Hamilton (Ontario) in 1905.[167] By means of a poem she had written a sister not only instructed the students in prescribed chemistry topics, but also taught them to be extremely cautious about the advances of the boys!

To determine the way in which congregational girls' schools in the Canadian province of New Brunswick in the second half of the 19th century encouraged nationalism, Sheila Andrew made a comparison with the classical male colleges conducted by male orders.[168] Whereas the latter encouraged a more aggressive Acadian, Québécois, and Irish nationalism as a valued manifestation of masculine emulation, the convent schools for girls seem to have promoted a rather apolitical nationalism, which was based more upon "Catholic pride in surviving persecution and establishing unity in religion that included the heritage and language of Québécois, Irish, and Acadian pupils".[169]

As regards extra-curricular sports activities in Catholic secondary schools in the Dutch city of Nijmegen in the first half of the 20th century, Marjet Derks drew attention to the considerable difference which existed between an Ursuline girls' school and a Jesuit boys' college.[170] In the former the sports culture was much more modest than in the latter. Moderate physical exercise was considered recommendable, but more exuberant sports, special trophies and competition with other girls' teams were regarded as inappropriate. The physical culture of the school was mild compared with that at the boys' college, but it was rather progressive compared to that of other Catholic girls' schools at the same time. Derks connected this with the personality of the principal and believed that the latter strategically used the excellent sports facilities of the school to set the institution apart from the many schools for Catholic girls.

Educational practice

In the 1990s several prominent historians of education made a plea to pay more attention to educational praxis within the classroom.[171] Despite the notable rise of such 'classroom history', this new trend has hardly influenced the study of the educational work of women religious so far.

Some articles which deal with a particular teaching congregation include a short discussion of the everyday practices of schooling,[172] but in-depth analyses of what actually happened within the classrooms of the nuns do not seem to exist.

Some interesting comments have been made about the way teaching sisters disciplined their pupils. In a general study about the disciplining of Canadian children between 1930 and 1960 Mona Gleason pointed out that teaching nuns had a dual authority at school.[173] Besides the authority of their rank as teachers and rightful heads of the class, they also had religious authority. When they punished a pupil, such punishment had the "additional aura of religious sanction".[174] She also cited evidence which illustrates that the teacher-nun had immense power over her children: the nun asked its fellow pupils to completely ignore a child who had repeatedly interrupted the class and this severe punishment had to last for a whole month, both in school and outside.

Thomas O'Donoghue put forward the interesting hypothesis that the stern approaches to discipline, obedience and respect for received doctrine had their origin in the way in which the teaching sisters had themselves been educated during their novitiate and in the treatment which the sisters themselves received from their superiors in the cloister.[175] The humiliations to which some female pupils were subjected by nuns in the presence of their peers possibly mirror the experience which those same teachers had had at the hands of their mistresses of novices. In the instructions of the Sisters of Mercy it is clearly written: "The proud and pretentious must be humbled by occasionally assigning to them the meanest employments …". O'Donoghue also pointed out that the common practice in many girls' boarding schools whereby the letters which the pupils sent or received were first read by one of the teachers might have been inspired by the inspection of the personal correspondence of the sisters by the mother superior.

Canadian scholars have spearheaded the study of the use of educational media by sisters in the classroom. Claire Rhéaume drew attention to the existence of more than 700 musical works which were composed for pedagogical use by the sisters of three Montreal orders.[176] We have already referred to a study by Christine Lei in which she describes how a sister in the Loretto Academy in

Hamilton (Ontario), an upper-middle class high school for girls administered by the Institute of the Blessed Virgin Mary, made use of a poem in her 1905 science class.[177] In line with the new education movement which advised teachers to relate the educational content of their lessons to the life experience of the pupils, the sister had composed a poem about a ball in which scientific nomenclature and chemical properties were intertwined with the students' interests in boys and dances. The poem, which was intended to be sung, functioned as a modern pedagogical mnemonic device.

Elizabeth Smyth observed that the religious teaching orders specifically instructed their members in the use of readers and other textbooks, and that a close scrutiny of the congregational texts, e.g. constitutions and plans of study, might improve our understanding of how school books were actually used in the classroom.[178]

The use of objects to illustrate lessons on natural sciences and the development of school museums in the girls' boarding schools of the *Soeurs des Saints Noms de Jésus et de Marie* in Quebec were the subject of a pioneering article by Dominique Laperle.[179]

Finally, Willemijn Ruberg's study on the use of children's correspondence as a pedagogical tool in the Netherlands between 1770 and 1850 has the merit of drawing attention to the fact that nuns sometimes dictated fictional letters containing admonitions and advice.[180]

Life and the lived experience of teachers and students

Despite the revival of 'life histories' in the history of education,[181] biographies of women religious involved in education are not very numerous and, as we pointed out earlier, biographical compendia on the history of education rarely contain entries about them.[182] The existing biographical studies primarily deal with sisters in leadership positions, such as the founders and first superiors general of orders,[183] later superiors general,[184] mothers superior of individual houses,[185] principals,[186] and sister-professors.[187] Also sisters who played a pioneering role in the development of particular domains such as special education,[188] vocational training[189] and language instruction for adults[190] have been the subject of biographies. It is striking that the 'ordinary' teaching sister is almost completely ignored in biographical research.

In most of the biographies the educational contribution of the person whose life has been studied is only one of many subjects dealt with. An exception is the recent study of Cornelia Connelly by Roseanne McDougall.[191] She portrayed Connelly, the founder of the Society of the Holy Child Jesus, as an innovator who revolutionized the school curriculum for girls in mid-19th century England. Apart from giving a detailed description of Connelly's work in education between 1846 and 1864, the first eighteen years of the Society, she reconstructed the process through which Connelly arrived at her educational synthesis.

The quality of the life history studies is uneven, serious treatises appearing alongside works without any historical pretensions.[192] Despite assertions that biographies tend to be hagiographical rather than analytical, real hagiography is certainly no longer as common as it used to be.[193] Occasionally, however, a hagiographical tone can still be encountered in works written by members of religious communities.

It has been observed that in the history of education there is a need for collective biographies,[194] and this certainly also applies to the study of women religious educators. While there are several synchronic and diachronic group biographies of lay women teachers,[195] it is still rare to find similar works dealing with teaching sisters. One example of a collective biography is Jenny Collins's study of the lives of a group of eight New Zealand born Dominican Sisters who worked in primary and secondary schools from the 1930s until the 1960s. Though her MA thesis on the subject remains unpublished,[196] some of her findings are incorporated in two refreshing articles. In one she looked at the life histories of the sisters in general.[197] Her analysis confirms Kathleen Weiler's thesis that women represent themselves in ambiguous stories: on the one hand, they accept the expectations of the dominant discourses about women of their generation and, on the other hand, they rebel against them. Women religious did not directly challenge the power, structural and material constraints of life as a Dominican teaching sister, but they seem to have developed four strategies which enabled them to combine teaching and religious life successfully: (1) 'compliance strategies' which allowed them to 'fit in' to convent life and to acquire the basics of teaching; (2) 'negotiation strategies' which enabled them to solve problems, to deal with people in positions of authority and to meet the educational needs of their pupils; (3) 'resistance strategies' which they followed when they felt it necessary for the good of the pupils and (4) several strategies which taught them to take the initiative and which made them deal with situations which required a flexible approach to problem solving. Collins's findings clearly show that "behind the face-obscuring veil and the habit" there are "individual women with personalities".[198]

In the other article Collins specifically explored the experience of the eight Dominican sisters as school principals, utilising Foucault's concept of power.[199] She found that many sisters spoke in a deprecatory way about their leadership and often attributed their appointment as principal to chance factors such as the illness of a colleague rather than to their own abilities. Collins connected this with the convent ethos to avoid pride in one's accomplishments and also with a certain need to apologize for intruding into what was perceived as 'the male world of leadership'. The narratives of the sisters clearly show that membership of a religious community provided exceptional opportunities but also brought oppressive constraints. Unlike most of the women in the world outside the convent, sisters could obtain a leadership position and wield considerable power. On the other hand, they were subject to the authority of both the convent rule and the Church hierarchy and they lived in an environment which promoted the virtues of self-effacement, compliance and obedience. Sometimes sisters ignored the convent rules when they felt that this was necessary to enable them to assert their full authority as leaders of the school and some of them were able masterfully to negotiate with the bishop. She concluded: "the women are revealed not as docile bodies but as capable of challenging and resisting the structures of domination in their lives".

By means of an analysis of obituaries, Stephanie Burley assessed the leadership qualities exhibited by the principals of some of the secondary girls' schools administered by the Dominicans and Sisters of Mercy in South Australia from 1880 to 1925.[200] Fully aware of the celebratory nature of such sources, she has used them only for information relating to the intellectual background, professional training and educational achievements of the sisters. She made a distinction between principals who founded a local institute or a school ('founding principals') and principals who directed the establishment at a later period ('later principals'), and by discussing both categories with specific examples, she highlighted the breadth of management and fiscal skills these women possessed. Like Collins, she noticed a major paradox inherent in their lifestyle. On the one hand, their membership of a religious order gave them the chance to escape from the subordination and limitations experienced by women outside the convent: the many schools established by the congregations offered the sisters exceptional opportunities for independence of thought and action. On the other hand, they were required to fulfill the vow of obedience and had to submit to the rules of the community, instructions from the mother general and the local bishop's attempts to interfere. Although Burley stressed that we should not declare these principals 'the superwomen of the late 19th and early 20th centuries', she also pointed out that "their roles were more complex, more dynamic, and more influential than much of the rhetoric and some of the earlier analyses would have us believe".

Jacqueline Gresko studied archival documents to compare the lives and careers of the Sisters of St. Ann and the Oblate Brothers who taught in three parallel sets of schools and missions in British Columbia (Canada) in 1881.[201] Her research strongly nuances the popular and stereotypic image that these religious worked as 'serfs' in a repressive hierarchical system administered by priests and bishops. Both communities indeed served in a hierarchical Church, but they did not completely lack agency, recognition, or respect. The sisters were not only able to negotiate on their own terms with the male hierarchy, they also had the opportunity to network with other women religious (e.g. the Grey Nuns) and with lay women. The Oblate Brothers had less latitude for negotiation than the sisters.

Kathleen Casey concentrated on the life histories of three groups of activist women teachers working in five cities in the north eastern US in the second half of the 20th century.[202] Besides the narratives of secular Jewish and black women teachers, her study also includes those of Catholic women religious who taught in parochial schools and who worked for social change and justice. It is praiseworthy that the author has 'given voice' to ordinary women teachers of a category largely neglected by existing scholarship, but as the individual stories triumph over the group perspective, she has not completely succeeded in determining the group discourse and producing a collective biography.[203]

Thérèse Hamel followed an 'autobiographical narrative approach' to reconstruct the way people experienced the abolition of normal schools and the transfer of teacher training to universities in the late 1960s in Quebec, but her study is rather unspecific with regard to the experiences of the nuns teaching in the normal schools at the time.[204]

Whereas interviews or written questionnaires can provide useful information on the lives and experiences of teaching sisters from the more recent periods,[205] so-called 'egodocuments' such as diaries, memoirs, autobiographies and correspondence are indispensable for studying the 'life histories' of the sisters in the more distant past. There are some editions of such writings, in the first place the correspondence of foundresses,[206] and a few specific studies have been undertaken regarding such documents. One example is Victoria Cohen Imarch's analysis of a corpus of letters written by a teaching order in Argentina to the ecclesiastical and civil authorities on the occasion of the educational reforms and the secularization process in the second half of the 19th century.[207] In general, however, Margaret MacCurtain's appeal to allow the voices of women religious to be heard,[208] to let them speak through their own words, does not seem to have had a big impact in the field of the history of education. Whereas several collections and studies exist about the autobiographical writings of 19th century male teachers[209] and Sharif Gemie has produced an interesting work which aims to listen to the voices of secular schoolmistresses of 19th century France,[210] analogous works relating to teaching sisters are completely lacking. Because the personal writings of a sister were usually destroyed in the convent after her death, much 'detective work' will be needed to locate the few autobiographical documents which have survived.

Studies on the experiences of girls schooled by sisters further help to refine our view of the educational activities and methods of the women religious.[211] To reconstruct the daily life of Catholic boarding schools in Holland and Flanders between 1920 and 1965, Marieke Hilhorst interviewed nineteen ex-students.[212] Her primary aims were to find out what it was like to be educated in a convent boarding school, what daily life was like, what the contacts were with other students and the sisters and what value the interviewees assigned retrospectively to their school life. Her research is not a rigorous scientific study of the phenomenon of Catholic boarding schools, but it provides a good atmospheric description of what life in such boarding schools was like.

For their important book on girls educated in a convent boarding school and on the education provided in such an establishment, a group of Canadian scholars also partially used oral history.[213] In a contribution to this work, Nadia Fahmy-Eid made the important point that it is not possible to hear the voice of pupils through the school newspapers because these were controlled, censored and even partly written by the school authorities. One of the editors of the book, Micheline Dumont, has recently published a vivid description of her own time at the boarding school of the *Soeurs de Sainte-Anne* in the town of Vaudreuil in Quebec during the late 1940s and early 1950s.[214]

Jackie Bennett and Rosemary Forgan edited an interesting collection of personal reminiscences of women who received their education from teaching sisters.[215] The women talk about what most affected their early lives, from spirituality to sexuality. The book shows a wide range of experiences: whereas some girls had a terrible time, others look back more positively upon it.[216] Some remember inspiring teachers and eccentric role models. Other girls testify to remarkable freedoms, such as being allowed to read erotic Latin poetry from a locked cupboard. The memories of girls who were educated in Irish convent schools seem generally somewhat more negative.

A large-scale study of the memoirs and autobiographies of former students, such as the one undertaken regarding the male pupils of the classical colleges in Quebec in 1880-1939,[217] might be useful to map the experiences and perceptions of the pupils in earlier periods.[218]

The professionalization of teaching

Raymond Grew and Patrick Harrigan saw secularization as "a part of the trend toward higher standards and professionalization",[219] and Philippe Savoie, Annie Bruter and Willem Frijhoff claimed that secularization was even one of the conditions of the professionalization of teaching.[220] Paul Wynants observed that with the secularization and bureaucratization of the educational sector, teaching appeared less "comme un champ d'apostolat, mais davantage comme un métier requérant connaissances techniques et expérience professionnelle".[221] Such statements seem to suggest that the large number of teaching sisters affected the professionalization of teaching in a negative way.

However, several studies have demonstrated how much the secular schools in 19th century France borrowed from the teaching orders: the curricula and teaching methods,[222] the values and corporate identity which were instilled into the new lay women teachers,[223] the strict rulings on which life in lay boarding schools was modelled, as well as the physical organization of schools.[224] So, it would be a gross oversimplification to state that government-organized secularization and bureaucratization eventually professionalized the educational sector which had been amateurishly organized by the religious orders for far too long. In fact, it seems fair to recognize that the professionalization of teaching owes much to the pedagogical experience and expertise of the teaching orders.

Our review of the literature has further demonstrated that sufficient attention has to be paid to developments over time and that the role of sisters in the professionalization of teaching has to be studied from multiple angles. In the present section we will discuss the following aspects: the training, competence and experience of sisters, their life-long career and career patterns, their specialization and corporate identity, their relationship with associations and unions of teachers, and, finally, their involvement in textbook production.

Training, competence and experience

Several scholars have nuanced the image of poorly trained and incompetent women religious teachers,[225] and Carmen Mangion has even gone a step further by portraying them as real professionals.[226]

Two reasons have been adduced to explain the negative, almost caricatural image of the unqualified teaching sister. First, there is the impact of anti-clerical or anti-Catholic historiography. This is especially the case in France where the republican historiography has underrated the contribution of the teaching orders by spotlighting the role of the state in the provision of schooling.[227] In the United States, the Protestant rhetoric in the sources has obscured the competence of Catholic teaching sisters and many historians have taken these negative statements at face value.[228]

The second reason is the religious dimension of the work of sisters.[229] The emphasis which was placed on piety and self-effacement obscured the technical skills of their work. As Annemieke van Drenth and Mineke van Essen put it: "a nun was never allowed to be proud of her knowledge or skills, which were only 'borrowed from God'".[230]

The studies clearly show that the teaching orders actively sought to improve the quality of the education they provided. First, they made considerable efforts to meet the state requirements of certification.[231] The community leaders and the superior directresses of studies often encouraged their members to pass government teaching examinations. Sometimes the teaching orders anticipated legislation about teaching certification and introduced teacher training well before the State intervened.[232]

Secondly, the orders carefully selected the sisters who were destined to be teachers: one had to meet certain qualifications in order to become a teaching sister. Novices who lacked aptitude for teaching were often encouraged to leave and some superiors general followed a policy to promote women with unquestionable teaching qualifications.[233]

Thirdly, the teaching communities, especially the 'director' or 'inspector' of studies, took special measures to help teaching sisters advance in both teaching methodology and knowledge of educational content. Starting teachers were mentored by more experienced teachers and they were also encouraged to improve their skills by private study. Moreover, the superior directresses of studies provided them constantly with recommendations on literature and materials. Extra training was organized through lectures, conferences, seminars, institutes, and even conventions for teaching sisters. Not only did lay women teachers have to do without the mentoring practice which was, in a manner of speaking, 'institutionalized' by the community life of women religious, but lay educators originally also had fewer opportunities to follow additional training programmes. Describing the summer courses which the *maîtresse des études* of the Congregation of Notre Dame organized for the teaching sisters in the mother house in Quebec in the early 1880s, Marta Danylewycz observed that it would be another thirty years before lay teachers would have a similar opportunity to polish up their teaching skills in Montreal's *Institut pédagogique*.[234]

Fourthly, teaching congregations sometimes introduced important educational reforms on their own initiative. The example discusssed by Clinton White is revealing in this regard as it illustrates how critically one has to approach the sources.[235] Whereas in a famous speech Reverend Edmund H. Oliver presented a very negative picture of the elementary schools of German Catholics in St. Peter's Colony in the province of Saskatchewan in Canada during and immediately following World War I, White has amply demonstrated that Oliver intentionally portrayed the education organized by the non-Anglo-Celtic population in a bad light to ensure that the provincial government would adopt a policy of 'English only' in all elementary schools. In doing so, Oliver and subsequent investigators left unmentioned the fact that at least six important educational reforms were in the process of being, or were soon to be implemented by the German Ursulines in their schools.

Some scholars have drawn attention to the sometimes already age-old educational traditions and teaching experiences within the orders.[236] Francis O'Hagan referred in this regard to the explanation which James Handley, a Marist Brother, offered of why members of religious orders were such effective teachers.[237] As it applies equally well to the female religious, we quote it in full: "[t]he section of their Rule that dealt with the art of instruction in all its ramifications was the product of years of experimental work, garnered from members of their Societies engaged in teaching in various parts of the world, and the periodic revision of such pedagogic material at their general Chapters, attended by delegates from all Provinces, ensured a deletion of all that outlived its usefulness and an admission of what had justified approbation. Their communal way of life and their unity of work and outlook rendered easy an interchange of ideas and a pooling for the benefit of all of methods of teaching that had proved effective".

So, when one takes into account all the evidence discussed so far, it has to be recognized that at least in certain periods some of the orders represented highly organized centres of pedagogical expertise.

The sisters involved in early childhood education, special education and nursing training also followed the trend toward more professionalization. For 19th century France, Jean-Noël Luc pointed out that several religious communities which were very active in providing day care for pre-school children in the so-called *salles d'asile* organized normal courses and published specialized guidebooks to run such institutions (for example Sister Maria's *Nouveau manuel des salles d'asile à l'usage des Filles de la Charité* from 1854 has almost 700 pages!).[238] Andrée Désilets has described how Albine Gadbois, a Sister of Providence known as Marie de Bonsecours, the foundress and first directress of the *Institution des sourdes-muettes de Montréal*, could stay abreast of the newest scientific developments in the field of education for the deaf.[239] In 1853-1854 she spent a year at the Peet Institution (New York School for the Deaf) and returned with new theoretical and practical knowledge. In 1870 she went to Europe to study a method of teaching which had been developed in Germany. During the same period of study leave she visited institutions similar to her own in Belgium, France, England, and Ireland.[240] Barbra Mann Wall demonstrated how Catholic sisters in the US between 1890 and 1920 brought their age-old involvement in nursing into line with modern society by establishing nursing training schools for both religious and secular women.[241] She pointed out that they not only adopted accepted standards of professionalization, but also stamped their own understanding of nursing onto secular society. Esther Lamontagne and Yolande Cohen recently argued that the theoretical knowledge of nursing which the Grey Nuns passed on to their students at the Quebec universities in the first half of the 20th century was directly derived from the practical knowledge which the nuns had acquired as administrators in the major hospitals.[242]

Life-long career and career patterns

Several scholars have pointed out that teaching sisters usually had a life-long career in teaching, whereas most of their lay counterparts taught only temporarily between their own schooling and their lives as wives and mothers.[243] Rebecca Rogers stated: "The teaching nun, married to Christ and completely devoted to her vocation, presented a powerful competing image to that of the lay schoolmistress".[244] So, it seems that the life-long involvement of sisters contributed more to the professionalization of the occupation than the constant coming and going of young lay women.

As a career ladder is generally recognized as a necessary precondition to professionalization, researchers should also pay attention to the career opportunities of women religious educators. Without explicitly relating it to the issue of the professionalization of the teaching profession, several scholars have observed that there were a wide variety of administrative and teaching positions for sisters, both within the convent and the schools of which the congregation was in charge: superior general, assistant to the superior general, member of the mother superior's council, secretary-general, local superior, assistant superior, mistress of novices, mistress of lay sisters, mistress of the school, mistress in charge of studies (presiding over all the teaching staff), mistress of boarders, specialized teachers for the upper grades, teachers for the lower grades, ...[245] So, unlike most of their lay counterparts who could not escape the socially imposed limitations on their gender, sisters had many opportunities for promotion and leadership in their self-managed institutions.

Scholars have started to study the career patterns of lay women teachers,[246] but similar research on female teachers in congregations is still lagging behind. In her study on the small French teaching order *Congrégation de la Mère de Dieu* Rebecca Rogers adduced a few examples of women who rose through the hierarchy.[247] Marta Danylewycz looked somewhat more closely at the career opportunities of the *Sœurs de la Congrégation de Notre-Dame* in Quebec between 1840 and 1920.[248] She found that women from upper- and middle-class households were more likely to obtain leadership positions than those of lower social standing, but that capable women from working-class or farming backgrounds could also make it to the top.

In her monograph on the history of the *Académie Marie-Rose* in Montreal Marie-Paule Malouin examined the mobility of teaching staff.[249] She pointed out that it was the general administration of the congregation (*Soeurs des Saints Noms de Jésus et de Marie*) who decided which women would work when and where. She also noted that the frequent transfer of the sisters had a positive influence on their professional experience.

Specialization and corporate identity

Langlois's study showed that the 19th century female congregations in France contributed considerably to the specialization of the labour market of women since most of the congregations focused on education, health care or social agency.[250] With regard to the situation in Boston between 1870 and 1940, Mary J. Oates pointed out that when a religious community was put under pressure by the bishop to expand its chosen field of endeavour because the diocese was in need of such work, it often tried to ensure that the arrangement would be short-term and after some time it returned to its former specialty.[251] This clearly indicates that at least some of the communities were groups really specialized in providing education, and hence deserved the designation 'teaching orders'.

Stephanie Burley observed that the strict division of labour within the communities also contributed to the formation of a specialized workforce: with the domestic requirements being fulfilled by lay sisters, the choir sisters could focus entirely on the development of their spiritual life and on their professional teaching career.[252]

A strong group identity is another important factor in the formation of a professional corps. Rebecca Rogers remarked that "the very structure of the religious order, with its novitiate and its autonomy from outside interference, gave it more professional characteristics than the average lay boarding school."[253]

Relationship with associations and unions of teachers

Although the scholarship on the history of associations and unions of teachers is impressive, the relationship of such organizations with religious teaching orders has hardly been studied. Marîse Thivierge published an interesting study on the unionization of Catholic women teachers in Quebec between 1900 and 1959, but she ignored women religious teachers.[254] Was it common for teaching sisters to be members of such associations? How was membership organized? Such questions need to be addressed.

In her history of the important union of Catholic primary school teachers in Belgium *Christelijk Onderwijzers Verbond* (COV), Lies Van Rompaey showed that the *Zusters der Christelijke Scholen van Vorselaar*, a religious order which was heavily engaged in teacher training, could exert considerable pressure on the union, for example in the debate around the marriage ban on women teachers.[255] Her findings indicate that this is an interesting angle which deserves further study.

It is also little known that some women religious contributed to the foundation of a teachers' assocation. Sister Mary Teresa Dunlevie, the headmistress of a school of the Sisters of Mercy in South Australia from 1918 to 1944, was a founding member of the Catholic Teachers' Association, and Sister Mary Dorothea King, Prefect of Studies of the Sisters of St. Ann, founded in 1958 the British

Columbia Catholic Teachers' Association and became its first President.[256] More attention has to be paid to the role of women religious in the creation of and participation in professional networks.

Involvement in textbook production

The involvement of women religious in the production and diffusion of educational media like textbooks is another important indicator of the professionalization of their educational activities. Although *Schulbuchforschung* is currently a much-studied branch in the history of education, this specific topic has hitherto almost exclusively been explored by researchers from Quebec.

Paul Aubin recently demonstrated that between 1765 and 1964 religious communities of both men and women were responsible for the production of almost 45% of all textbooks in Quebec.[257] His findings nuance the widely held view, diffused by André Labarrère-Paulé since the 1960s, that it was the male lay teacher who, through his active role in textbook production, the pedagogical press and the teachers' associations, almost single-handedly professionalized teaching in the 19th century.[258]

In her detailed case study of the production of textbooks in Quebec by the *Sœurs de la Congrégation de Notre-Dame*, Thérèse Hamel addressed a new aspect of the study of the professional involvement of women religious in education.[259] She measured the extent of the production of pedagogical books, intended for either teachers or pupils, and she mapped the different disciplines covered by them. Through an examination of the number of editions they went through she tried to establish how long textbooks were in use and she identified the steady sellers of the congregation. She has also observed that the sisters were most productive in the decennia 1910-1919 and 1950-1959, and that there was a steep decline during the 1960s. She noted that in many cases textbooks were published anonymously, something which she associated with the fact that congregations encouraged the anonymity of their members. She stressed that more research is needed on the authors of these books and that similar studies on other religious communities are necessary to assess whether this particular congregation is unique in the production of textbooks.

In his study on the staffing and curriculum in Polish-American parochial schools, William Galush observed that in the 1930s the Felicians started to use more textbooks which had been produced within the community (he referred in particular to Sister M. Cyryla, a very prolific writer).[260] He regarded the involvement of those sisters in the preparation of curricular materials as a part of their growing professionalization after World War I.

Changes in the composition of the teaching staff

In his work *Le catholicisme au féminin* Claude Langlois made extensive use of quantitative sources, and this enabled him to map the increase in women religious teachers in France during the 19th century.[261] Apart from this landmark study, hardly any serious quantitative research has been undertaken on the process which Langlois designated as the '*cléricalisation*', '*sororisation*' or '*congrégationalisation de la fonction enseignante féminine*'.[262] As we have already pointed out, the extensive literature on the feminization of the teaching force in the late 19th and 20th centuries almost systematically ignores the very strong influx of women religious into the teaching profession.[263]

The counter-process, i.e. the laicization of the school staff, has likewise received scant scholarly attention. Marie-Paule Malouin made a quantitative study of the laicization of the public school in Quebec between 1939 and 1969 in which she came to the conclusion that this process was accompanied by a masculinization of leadership functions.[264] She argues that the situation in which women occupied these high positions was apparently so exceptional in history – one might almost say 'unnatural' – that it was again 'normalized'! David Stapleton examined the shift from religious order administration to lay administration in Catholic secondary schools in post-World War II Victoria (Australia).[265] His study includes some quantitative data, but follows a more qualitative approach.

Since this historiographical survey is a direct consequence of our research on the feminization of the teaching staff in Belgium, it is fitting to conclude with some observations and hypotheses regarding the impact of the educational involvement of women religious on the process of the feminization of teaching.

Alison Prentice and Marjorie Theobald rightly pointed to the problematic nature of the concept of 'feminization of teaching'.[266] The concept places too much emphasis on the mid-19th century transition to public schools and ignores the fact that women religious had been involved and had had lifetime careers in girls' education long before then. "In areas where Roman Catholic convent schools existed", they argued, "the feminization of state school teaching must be studied in the context of church/state relations and women's acceptance or rejection of religious vocations. In such societies, the relations between lay and religious teachers are an important part of the history of the occupation".

Stephanie Burley criticized the oversimplified notion in the history of education that 'women teach and men manage' because it completely ignores the fact that in schools run by women religious there was no such sexual division of labour.[267] Interestingly, the religious communities had their own division of labour: the lay sisters undertook the domestic tasks, whereas the choir sisters were involved in the more 'serious' occupations. Because the choir sisters were relieved of the 'familial' domestic duties, traditionally the domain of women, they could undertake the supposed 'male management' roles.

Martha Danylewycz, Beth Light and Alison Prentice put forward the hypothesis that the speed at which the feminization process occurred in a country or region might be related to the presence of an established tradition of women in teaching prior to the emergence of government supported schooling.[268] This means that in regions like Quebec, teaching may have feminized faster because there was a long-standing cultural tradition of teaching sisterhoods.

That the existence of a strong tradition of educational work by sisters intensified the feminization process was also suggested by Jo Burr Margadant.[269] She claimed that the long-standing involvement of women religious in girls' education left the authorities of the French Third Republic who launched a secularization campaign no option other than to put lay women in charge of girls' education.

According to Christina de Bellaigue, French lay women could occupy leadership positions in private boarding schools for girls in the 19th century because they could draw on the socially legitimate exercise of authority by women in religious orders.[270] If this is correct, the involvement of women religious in education contributed to a partial neutralization of the usual sexual division of labour in teaching.

CHAPTER 4

Conclusions

Since Elizabeth Smyth's statement in 1994 that "the research on the history of teaching sisters is just beginning",[271] studies about the subject have multiplied considerably and a start has been made to apply to it some of the newer methodologies of the history of education. The numerous case studies on teaching congregations and schools run by sisters provide an immense number of useful data which can form the basis for developing general theories, concepts and models. Likewise, the many 'national' and 'regional' syntheses about women religious in the 19th and 20th centuries which have appeared in the last twenty years can provide an important point of reference for the activities of the teaching sisters.

Despite this notable progress, there is still a long way to go. Since most of the specialized literature on women religious and education is descriptive and limited to a particular school, congregation, city or region, much more generalizing, comparative and explanatory studies are needed. To test general hypotheses it is also important that more studies start from a well-defined research question.

As a very large number of the books, articles and papers about teaching congregations have little to say on education in the narrow sense of the word, new studies will have to address the educational philosophy of the teaching congregations, the curricula provided in schools conducted by the sisters and everyday practices in classrooms.

More research is also needed to determine the influence of the Holy See on the teaching orders, for example the impact of the 'Counsel to teaching sisters' given by Pope Pius XII on 15 September 1951 during the 'First International Congress of Teaching Sisters' in Rome, as well as the effect of Vatican Council II (1962-1965) on the involvement of women religious in education.[272] Marie-Paule Malouin published an important report on the situation of the teaching sisters in Quebec in the 1980s on the basis of a written questionnaire which the *Association des religieuses enseignantes du Québec* (AREQ) had sent to its members,[273] but it has more the character of a historical source than a historical study.

Perhaps the most striking conclusion of our review of the literature is that a large majority of the studies paint the educational endeavours of women religious in very positive terms. Scholars have shown that the secondary schools administered by sisters provided high quality education with an academic and progressive curriculum, that the women were highly competent and qualified professionals, that they made a giant contribution to universal schooling and that they did not just play a passive role in a male-dominated world, but developed strategies to achieve their own objectives. In the more general literature on women religious, where a similar trend praising women religious for their work and independence can be recognized, this current of 'pro-woman', almost feminist, historiography has been criticized by some scholars.[274] Likewise, in the broader field of women's history, it has been pointed out that the search for female victims of male oppression which dominated the historiography of women in the 1980s should not be replaced by an optimistic historiography focusing on the agency and autonomy of women.[275] So, one has to be vigilant that in research on the contribution of women religious to education the old hagiographic history writing is not replaced by a modern variant.

In every case, we hope that this review of the literature will promote the production of critical and unbiased scholarship in which both the favourable and less favourable aspects of sisters' involvement in education are illuminated so that, ultimately, these forgotten women teachers can be restored to their rightful place in the history of education.

Notes

1. See M. DEPAEPE, H. LAUWERS & F. SIMON, *De feminisering van het leerkrachtencorps*, in: *Revue belge de philologie et d'histoire/Belgisch Tijdschrift voor Filologie en Geschiedenis*, 82:4 (2004), pp. 969-995; M. DEPAEPE, H. LAUWERS & F. SIMON, *The Feminization of the Teaching Profession in Belgium in the Nineteenth and Twentieth Centuries*, in: R. CORTINA & S. SAN ROMAN (eds.), *Women and Teaching. Global Perspectives on the Feminization of a Profession*, New York, Palgrave, 2006, pp. 155-183; M. DEPAEPE, H. LAUWERS, F. SIMON, B. HELLINCKX & L. VAN ROMPAEY, *Mapa de la Feminización de la Enseñanza Primaria en Bélgica*, in: *Tempora: Revista de Sociología de la Educación*, 10 (2007), pp. 87-114.

2. See e.g. M.H. STROBER & A.G. LANFORD, *The Feminization of Public School Teaching: Cross-Sectional Analysis, 1850-1880*, in: *Signs: Journal of Women in Culture & Society*, 11 (1986), pp. 212-235; J. PERLMANN & R.A. MARGO, *Women's Work? American Schoolteachers, 1650-1920*, Chicago, University of Chicago Press, 2001; S. SAN ROMÁN GAGO, *La incorporación de la maestra a la escuela pública en España 1783-1882*, Cuadernos del Centro, México, El Colegio de San Luis, 2001.

3. F.M. PERKO, *Religious Schooling in America: An Historiographical Reflection*, in: *History of Education Quarterly*, 40:3 (2000), pp. 320-338, esp. pp. 323, 330-332, 337.

4. T. O'DONOGHUE & A. POTTS, *Researching the Lives of Catholic Teachers who were Members of Religious Orders: Historiographical Considerations*, in: *History of Education*, 33:4 (2004), pp. 469-481.

5. R. ROGERS, *L'éducation des filles: un siècle et demi d'historiographie*, in: P. CASPARD, J.-N. LUC & R. ROGERS (eds.), *L'éducation des filles XVIIIe-XXIe siècles. Hommage à Françoise Mayeur*, special issue of *Histoire de l'éducation*, vol. 115-116 (2007), pp. 37-79, esp. pp. 56-62.

6. E. KOLMER, *Catholic Women Religious and Women's History: A Survey of the Literature*, in: *American Quarterly*, 30:5 (1978) [= special Issue *Women and Religion*], pp. 639-651; G. LAPERRIÈRE, *Table ronde: "L'historiographie des congrégations religieuses: approches actuelles"*, in: *SCHEC Études d'histoire religieuse*, 57 (1990), pp. 21-27; M. DUMONT, *Une perspective féministe dans l'histoire des congrégations de femmes*, in: *SCHEC Études d'histoire religieuse*, 57 (1990), pp. 29-35; E. KOLMER, *Women Religious in the United States: A Survey of Recent Literature*, in: C. KAUFFMAN (ed.), *Women Religious: Historical Explorations* (special issue of *U.S. Catholic Historian*, 10:1-2), New York, United States Catholic Historical Society, 1992, pp. 87-92; J. EIJT, *Verborgen vrouwen, vergeten vrouwen? Veranderende visies op de geschiedenis van negentiende-eeuwse zustercongregaties*, in: *Trajecta: tijdschrift voor de geschiedenis van het katholiek leven in de Nederlanden*, 1 (1992), pp. 374-387; M. MACCURTAIN, *Late in the Field: Catholic Sisters in Twentieth-Century Ireland and the New Religious History*, in: J. HOFF & M. COULTER (eds.), *Irish Women's Voices Past and Present* (special issue of *Journal of Women's History* vols. 6-7), Bloomington (Ind.), Johns Hopkins University Press, 1995, pp. 49-63; J. VAN VUGT, *De geschiedenis van zusters, paters en broeders. Geschiedschrijving over het religieuze leven in Nederland in de laatste twee eeuwen: Resultaten tot nu toe en wensen voor de toekomst*, in: *Jaarboek Katholiek*

Documentatie Centrum, 26 (1997), pp. 126-63; P. WYNANTS, *Les religieuses de vie active en Belgique et aux Pays-Bas, 19e-20e siècles*, in: *Revue d'Histoire Ecclésiastique*, 95:3 (2000) [= special issue *Deux mille ans d'histoire de l'Église. Bilan et perspectives historiographiques*], pp. 238-256; G. LAPERRIÈRE, *Les communautés religieuses au Québec: pour une approche par familles spirituelles*, in: *SCHEC Études d'histoire religieuse*, 67 (2001), pp. 167-182; E.M. SMYTH, *Writing the History of Women Religious in Canada (1996-2001)*, in: *International Journal of Canadian Studies/Revue internationale d'études canadiennes*, 23 (2001), pp. 207-213; P. WYNANTS, *België en Nederland op gescheiden wegen? Geschiedschrijving van vrouwelijke congregaties 1990-2000*, in: *Trajecta: tijdschrift voor de geschiedenis van het katholiek leven in de Nederlanden*, 11:1 (2002), pp. 65-75; M. DERKS & J. EIJT, *Wie kookte het laatste avondmaal? Over de zichtbaarheid van vrouwen in religiegeschiedenis*, in: M. ACKERMANS & T. HOOGBERGEN (eds.), *Kloosters en religieus leven: Historie en toekomst*, 's-Hertogenbosch, Heijnen, 2003, pp. 194-203; J. DE MAEYER, S. LEPLAE & J. SCHMIEDL (eds.), *Religious Institutes in Western Europe in the 19th and 20th Centuries. Historiography, Research and Legal Position* (KADOC Studies on Religion, Culture & Society, 2), Leuven, Leuven University Press, 2004 (with contributions providing an overview of the research on male and female orders in Belgium, the Netherlands, France, Great Britain, Ireland, Germany and Switzerland); C.K. COBURN, *An Overview of the Historiography of Women Religious: A Twenty-Five-Year Retrospective*, in: *U.S. Catholic Historian*, 22:1 (2004), pp. 1-26; S. BURLEY, *An Overview of the Historiography of Women Religious in Australia*, in: *Journal of the Australian Catholic Historical Society*, 26 (2005), pp. 43-60; K. SUENENS & A.-D. MARCÉLIS, *Vrouwelijke religieuze instituten in België in de negentiende en twintigste eeuw. Een historiografisch overzicht*, in: M. VAN DIJCK, J. DE MAEYER & M.-E. HENNEAU (eds.), *Historiografie en onderzoeksperspectieven van ordes en congregaties op het grondgebied van de Zuidelijke Nederlanden/België*, special issue of *Revue belge de philologie et d'histoire/Belgisch Tijdschrift voor Filologie en Geschiedenis*, 86:4 (2008).

7. See e.g. T.W. CAMPBELL, *The Sisters of the Church and the Anglican Diocese of Sydney, 1892-1893: A Controversy*, in: *The Journal of Religious History*, 25:2 (2001), pp. 188-206; R. KOLLAR, *Flowers, Pictures, and Crosses: Criticisms of Priscilla Lydia Sellon's Care of Young Girls*, in: *Anglican Theological Review*, 86 (2004), pp. 451-471. For the role which Protestant women communities played in girls' and women's education in Germany see J. JACOBI, *"Entzauberung der Welt" oder "Rettung der Welt". Mädchen- und Frauenbildung im 19. Jahrhundert in Deutschland*, in: *Zeitschrift für Erziehungswissenschaft*, 9:2 (2006), pp. 177-180.

8. L. CADA et al., *Shaping the Coming Age of Religious Life*, New York, Seabury, 1979.

9. See e.g. A. BIANCHI & G. ROCCA (eds.), *L'educazione femminile tra cinque e settecento*, in: *Annali di Storia dell'Educazione e delle Istituzioni Scolastiche*, 14 (2007), pp. 11-176 (including historiographical overviews of Italy, Germany and Belgium); E. RAPLEY, *A Social History of the Cloister: Daily Life in the Teaching Monasteries of the Old Regime*, Montreal, McGill-Queen's University Press, 2001; L. LUX-STERRITT, *Redefining Female Religious Life: French Ursulines and English Ladies in Seventeenth-Century Catholicism*, Aldershot, Ashgate, 2005 (paying attention to "the birth of the new phenomenon of the teaching nun"); L. LUX-STERRITT, *Between the Cloister and the World: the Successful Compromise of the Ursulines of Toulouse, 1604-1616*, in: *French History*, 16:3 (2002), pp. 247-268; P. ANNAERT, *Les collèges au féminin. Les Ursulines: enseignement et vie consacrée aux XVIIe et XVIIIe siècles*, Namur, Vie consacrée, 1992; C. ROBENSTINE, *French Colonial Policy and the Education of Women and Minorities: Louisiana in the Early Eighteenth Century*, in: *History of Education Quarterly*, 32:2 (1992), pp. 193-211 (on the origins of the Ursuline Academy of New Orleans); A. DURET, *Les communautés religieuses*

enseignantes et missionnaires à Luçon aux XVIIe-XVIIIe siècles, Lille, A.N.R.T, Université de Lille III, 1996; B. DOMPNIER & M.-H. FROESCHLÉ-CHOPARD (eds.*), Les religieux et leurs livres à l'époque moderne. Actes du colloque de Marseille, EHESS, 2 et 3 avril 1997* (Collection Histoires croisées), Clermont-Ferrand, Presses universitaires Blaise-Pascal, 2000; V. CASTAGNET, *La formation religieuse reçue par les soeurs des congrégations enseignantes: une évidence pour les ursulines de Belgique, France et Nouvelle-France aux XVIIe et XVIIIe siècles?*, Paper presented at the *Journée d'études 'Religion, fait religieux et laïcité dans la formation des enseignants (XVIe-XXe siècles)'*, Lille, 14 November, 2008; M. DE VROEDE, *Religieuses et béguines enseignantes dans les Pays-Bas méridionaux et la Principauté de Liège aux XVIIe-XVIIIe siècles* (Studia Paedagogica 20), Leuven, Leuven University Press, 1996; A. RUTZ, *Bildung - Konfession - Geschlecht. Religiöse Frauengemeinschaften und die katholische Mädchenbildung im Rheinland (16. - 18. Jahrhundert)*, Mainz, von Zabern, 2006; L. MÖLLER, *Höhere Mädchenschulen in der Kurpfalz und im fränkischen Raum im 18. Jahrhundert* (Mainzer Studien zur Neueren Geschichte 5), Frankfurt am Main, Peter Lang 2001; G. WEIGAND, *Die weiblichen Schulorden und die Mädchenbildung*, in: J.G. PRINZ VON HOHENZOLLERN & M. LIEDTKE (eds.), *Der weite Schulweg der Mädchen. Die Geschichte der Mädchenbildung als Beispiel der Geschichte anthropologischer Fehlurteile* (Schriftenreihe zum Bayerischen Schulmuseum Ichenhausen), Bad Heilbrunn, Klinkhardt, 1990, pp. 127-147; G. WEIGAND, *Die weiblichen Schulorden*, in: M. LIEDTKE (ed.), *Handbuch der Geschichte des bayerischen Bildungswesens*, Bad Heilbrunn, Klinkhardt, 1991, vol. 1, pp. 605-621; C. BOWDEN, *"For the Glory of God": a Study of the Education of English Catholic Women in Convents in Flanders and France in the First Half of the Seventeenth Century*, in: J. COOLAHAN, R. ALDRICH & F. SIMON (eds.), *Faiths and Education: Historical and Comparative Perspectives* (*Paedagogica Historica* Supplementary Series 5), Gent, CSHP, 1999, pp. 77-95; C. BOWDEN, *Community Space and Cultural Transmission: Formation and Schooling in English Enclosed Convents in the Seventeenth Century*, in: *History of Education*, 34:4 (2005), pp. 365-386; C. SCHILLINGER-PRASSL, *"Die jungen Fräulein in allen guten Sitten und Tugenden zu unterweisen". Die weiblichen Schulorden in Österreich in der Frühen Neuzeit*, in: I. BREHMER & G. SIMON (eds.), *Geschichte der Frauenbildung und Mädchenerziehung in Österreich*, Graz, Leykam, 1997, pp. 92-102; A. CONRAD, *Weibliche Lehrorden und katholische höhere Mädchenschulen im 17. Jahrhundert*, in: E. KLEINAU & C. OPITZ (eds.), *Geschichte der Mädchen- und Frauenbildung*, vol. 1: *Vom Mittelalter bis zur Aufklärung*, Frankfurt, Campus, 1996, pp. 252-262; A. CONRAD, *Die weiblichen "Devoten" als Instrumente der konfessionellen Erziehung in Frankreich und Deutschland*, in: H. SCHILLING (ed.), *Spannungsfeld von Staat und Kirche. "Minderheiten" und "Erziehung" im deutsch-französischen Gesellschaftsvergleich. 16. - 18. Jahrhundert*, Berlin, Duncker & Humblot, 2003, pp. 191-214; M. SONNET, *L'éducation des filles au temps des Lumières*, Paris, Cerf, 1987; F. SOURY-LAVERGNE, *Chemin d'éducation: sur les traces de Jeanne de Lestonnac 1556-1640*, Chambray-lès-Tours, CLD, 1985; E. CLARK, *Masterless Mistresses: The New Orleans Ursulines and the Development of a New World Society, 1727-1834*, Chapel Hill, University of North Carolina Press, 2007; P.M. WATERS, *The Ursuline Achievement. A Philosophy of Education for Women. St. Angela Merici, the Ursulines and Catholic Education*, North Carlton, Colonna, 1994; A. DEL VALLE LÓPEZ, *La actividad educadora, directa e institucional: órdenes y congregaciones femeninas dedicadas a la enseñanza*, in: B. BARTOLOMÉ MARTÍNEZ (ed.), *Historia de la acción educadora de la iglesia en España*, I: *Edades Antigua, Media y Moderna* (Biblioteca de autores cristianos. Series maior 49), Madrid, Biblioteca de Autores Cristianos, 1995, pp. 723-745; M.L. BREY ALVAREZ, *Una educadora novohispana: María Ignacia de Azlor y Echeverz*, Bogotá, CELAM, 1989; P. FOZ Y FOZ, *Las enseñanzas iberoamericanas: 1754-1820*,

Bogotá, CELAM, 1988; R. RAUGHTER, *Pious Occupations: Female Activism and the Catholic Revival in Eighteenth-Century Ireland*, in: R. RAUGHTER (ed.), *Religious Women and their History: Breaking the Silence*, Dublin: Irish Academic Press, 2005 (primarily about Nano Nagle and Teresa Mulally who initiated education for poor children); M.P. O'FARRELL, *Nano Nagle, Woman of the Gospel*, Cork, Cork Publishing, 1996.

10. See e.g. R. ROGERS, *Constructing French Womanhood over the Seas: Religious Teaching Congregations and the Civilizing Mission in Africa and the United States in the Nineteenth Century*, Paper presented at the *XIXe Congrès international des sciences historiques*, Oslo, 2000; K. SHELDON, *"I Studied with the Nuns, Learning to Make Blouses": Gender Ideology and Colonial Education in Mozambique*, in: *The International Journal of African Historical Studies*, 31:3 (1998), pp. 595-625; R. CHRISTENS, *Terra incognita. 75 jaar annuntiaten in Afrika*, Tielt, Lannoo, 2006 [translation: *Terra incognita. 75 ans de présence annonciade en Afrique*, Tielt, Lannoo, 2006]; M. DEPAEPE & L. VAN ROMPAEY, *In het teken van de bevoogding. De educatieve actie in Belgisch-Kongo 1908-1960*, Leuven, Garant, 1995; M. DEPAEPE, F. DEBAERE & L. VAN ROMPAEY, *Missionary Education in the Belgian Congo during the Colonial Period (1908-1960)*, in: *Neue Zeitschrift für Missionswissenschaft/Nouvelle Revue de science missionaire*, 48:4 (1992), pp. 265-280.

11. See e.g. A. VAN DRENTH & M. VAN ESSEN, *The Ambiguity of Professing Gender: Women Educationists and New Education in the Netherlands (1890-1940)*, in: *Paedagogica Historica*, 44:4 (2008), pp. 379-396. Part of the article is devoted to Ida B.M. Frye (1909-2003), a nun in the congregation of the Daughters of Mary and Joseph, who did some pioneering research in the field of special education, especially on autism.

12. It is very common – and not a little frustrating – to find many references to unpublished MA or PhD theses. A bibliographical compendium on the history of education in Belgium up to 1986 gives an idea of how great the proportion of such works can be in comparison with the total scholarly output: 1/3 of the literature mentioned on female religious orders consists of theses: see M. DE VROEDE, J. LORY & F. SIMON, *Bibliographie de l'histoire de l'enseignement préscolaire, primaire, normal et spécial en Belgique 1774-1986*, Leuven, Acco, 1988, pp. 187-200.

13. *Boletín de Historia de la Educación* (Spain); *Educació i Història: Revista d'Història de l'Educació* (Spain: Catalonia), *Histoire de l'Éducation* (France), *Historia de la Educación* (Spain), *Historia de la Educación Anuario* (Argentina), *Historical Studies in Education/Revue d'histoire de l'éducation* (Canada), *History of Education* (United Kingdom), *History of Education Quarterly* (United States of America), *History of Education Review* (Australia & New Zealand), *History of Education Society Bulletin/History of Education Researcher* (United Kingdom), *Jaarboek voor de geschiedenis van opvoeding en onderwijs* (Belgium & the Netherlands), *Jahrbuch für Historische Bildungsforschung* (Germany), *Memoria, Conocimiento y Utopía: Anuario de la Sociedad Mexicana de Historia de la Educación* (Mexico), *Paedagogica Historica* (international), *Revista Brasileira de História da Educação* (Brazil), *Revista HISTEDBR On-line* (Brazil), *Revista Historia de la Educación Latinoamericana* (Latin America), *Sarmiento. Anuario Galego de Historia da Educación* (Spain: Galicia), *Tempora: Revista de Historia y Sociologia de la Educacion/Tempora: Revista de Sociología de la Educación* (Spain), *Zeitschrift für pädagogische Historiographie* (Switzerland).

14. See e.g. N. FAHMY-EID, *L'histoire de l'éducation des filles au Québec, la pointe de l'iceberg*, in: *Historical Studies in Education/Revue d'histoire de l'éducation*, 3:2 (1991), p. 220; J. ALEJO MONTES, *Review of I. Azcárate Rístori, El Monasterio de la Enseñanza de Barcelona, 1645-1876 (Barcelona, 1993)*, in: *Historia de la Educación*, 12-13 (1993-1994), p. 618; L. EISENMANN, *Reconsidering a Classic: Assessing the History of Women's Higher Education a Dozen Years after Barbara Solomon*, in: *Harvard Educational Review*, 67:4 (1997), pp. 693, 708; R. ROGERS,

Retrograde or Modern? Unveiling the Teaching Nun in Nineteenth-century France, in: *Social History*, 23:2 (1998), p. 149; Anon., *Book note of G. Ramis (ed.), I Simposium d'Historia social del segle XIX. Aproximació a Sor María Rafela del Sgt. Cor i al seu entorn religiós i històric (1814-1899), Caixa de Balears, 1999*, in: *Boletín de Historia de la Educación*, 32 (2000); S. HOY, *Review of C.K. Coburn & M. Smith, Spirited Lives: How Nuns Shaped Catholic Culture and American Life, 1836-1920 (Chapel Hill: University of North Carolina Press, 1999)*, in: *History of Education Quarterly*, 41:1 (2001), p. 101; E. SMYTH, *Preserving Habits: Memory within Communities of English Canadian Women Religious*, in: L.R. MCLEAN & K. O'ROURKE (eds.), *Framing Our Past: Canadian Women's History in the Twentieth Century*, Montreal, McGill-Queen's Press, 2001, p. 22; M. VAN ESSEN & R. ROGERS, *Écrire l'histoire des enseignantes. Enjeux et perspectives internationales*, in: *Histoire de l'éducation*, 98 (2003), p. 7; R. ROGERS, *La sous-maîtresse française au XIXe siècle: domestique ou enseignante stagiaire?*, in: *Histoire de l'éducation*, 98 (2003), p. 37; S. O'BRIEN, *A Survey of Research and Writing about Roman Catholic Women's Congregations in Great Britain and Ireland (1800-1950)*, in: DE MAEYER, LEPLAE & SCHMIEDL, *Religious Institutes in Western Europe* [see note 6], p. 99; O'DONOGHUE & POTTS, *Researching the Lives* [see note 4], p. 471; C.M. MANGION, *"Good Teacher" or "Good Religious"? The Professional Identity of Catholic Women Religious in Nineteenth-Century England and Wales*, in: *Women's History Review*, 14 (2005), p. 223; BURLEY, *An Overview of the Historiography of Women Religious* (see note 6), pp. 43-60; D. RAFTERY & C. NOWLAN-ROEBUCK, *Convent Schools and National Education in Nineteenth-Century Ireland: Negotiating a Place within a Non-Denominational System*, in: *History of Education*, 36:3 (2007), pp. 354-355.

15. E. SMYTH, *Loretto Academy Niagara (1861-1969): Education under the Rainbow*, in: *Encounters on Education*, 7 (2006), p. 27.

16. M.-M. COMPÈRE, *L'histoire de l'éducation en Europe: essai comparatif sur la façon dont elle s'écrit*, Paris, INRP, 1995, p. 273.

17. I. HAVELANGE, *Vingt ans de bibliographie d'histoire de l'éducation française (1979-1998)*, in: *Histoire de l'éducation*, 93 (2002), p. 83.

18. J. HERBST, *The History of Education: State of the Art*, in: *Paedagogica Historica*, 35 (1999), pp. 745-746.

19. The proceedings: *Les religieuses enseignantes XVI - XX siècles. Actes de la quatrième rencontre d'histoire religieuse organisée à Fontevraud le 4 octobre 1980 par le Centre de Recherche d'Histoire Religieuse et d'Histoire des Idées (Université d'Angers) et le Centre Culturel de l'Ouest, Université d'Angers* (Publications du Centre de recherches d'histoire religieuse et d'histoire des idées 4), Angers, Presses de l'Université d'Angers, 1981. This collection contains three relevant contributions: about the first 60 years of the *Sœurs de l'instruction chrétienne de Saint-Gildas-des-Bois* (by M. FAUGERAS: pp. 101-113), about the origin and foundation history of the *Société du Sacré-Cœur* (by J. DE CHARRY: pp. 127-135) and about the first female congregations in the United States in the first half of the 19th century (by C. LEMARIÉ: pp. 137-150). In his review of the book, C. LANGLOIS, *Archives des sciences sociales des religions* 54:2 (1982), p. 195, rightly observed that the conference acts "ne s'intéressent pas directement à l'enseignement".

20. *71e Congrès de la Société canadienne d'histoire de l'Église catholique: Communautés religieuses et éducation*, 24th and 25th September 2004. During the European Social Science History Conference in Amsterdam in March 2006 a session was held on 'Childhood in a Religious Setting'.

21. P. GORDON & R. ALDRICH, *Biographical Dictionary of North American and European Educationists*, London, The Woburn Press, 1997, p. 514 (Mary Evaline Wolff, 'Sister Madeleva').

22. A. PRENTICE & M.R. THEOBALD (eds.), *Women who Taught: Perspectives on the History of Women and Teaching*, Toronto, University of Toronto Press, 1991; M. VAN ESSEN & R. ROGERS (eds.), Les *enseignantes. Formations, identités, représentations XIXe-XXe siècles*, special issue of *Histoire de l'éducation*, vol. 98, 2003 (with contributions by the Standing Working Group on Gender of the 2002 ISCHE conference).

23. The 6 British educational activists who form the subject of J. MARTIN & J. GOODMAN, *Women and Education 1800-1980. Educational Reform and Personal Identities*, Basingstoke, Palgrave Macmillan, 2004, are all lay women. Likewise, hardly anything is said about teaching sisters in studies such as that of S. GEMIE, *Women and Schooling in France, 1815-1914. Gender, Authority and Identity in the Female Schooling Sector*, Keele, Keele University Press, 1995 (about secular schoolmistresses in 19th century France); D. COPELMAN, *London's Women Teachers: Gender, Class and Feminism, 1870-1930*, London, Routledge, 1996, and E. CORTADA ANDREU, *Ser mestra a la Catalunya del segle XIX. L'escola pública com a espai professional transgressor*, Lleida, Pagès editors, 2006.

24. See note 2.

25. For an overview of the literature on lay women teachers see A. PRENTICE & M.R. THEOBALD, *The Historiography of Women Teachers: A Retrospect*, in: PRENTICE & THEOBALD, *Women who Taught* (see note 22), pp. 3-33; VAN ESSEN & ROGERS, *Écrire l'histoire des enseignantes* (see note 14), pp. 5-35 [translation: *Zur Geschichte der Lehrerinnen: Historiographische Herausforderungen und internationale Perspektiven*, in: *Zeitschrift für Pädagogik*, 3 (2006), pp. 319-337].

26. C. CLEAR, *Nuns in Nineteenth Century Ireland*, Dublin, Gill & Macmillan, 1987, p. XVII.

27. J. SÉGUY, *Review of C. Langlois, Le catholicisme au féminin. Les congrégations françaises à supérieure générale au XIXe siècle (Paris: Cerf, 1984)*, in: *Archives des sciences sociales des religions*, 59:2 (1985), p. 275. For an extensive summary of the study see C. LANGLOIS, *Le Catholicisme au féminin*, in: *Archives des sciences sociales des religions*, 57:1 (1984), pp. 29-53.

28. For this three-stage model (pre-1950, 1950-1970, post-1970), first developed by H. de Valk with regard to the Netherlands and then generalized, see J. DE MAEYER, S. LEPLAE & J. SCHMIEDL, *Religious Institutes in Western Europe in the 19th and 20th Centuries: An Underrated History*, in: DE MAEYER, LEPLAE & SCHMIEDL, *Religious Institutes in Western Europe* (see note 6), pp. 7-26. Regarding the rise in interest, P. Wynants also pointed to the fact that many convents and congregations commissioned historical studies of their institutes on the occasion of important jubilees. Moreover, he noted that research groups at universities were realizing more and more that this topic had to be addressed since both access to archives and the ability to make use of oral interviews would decrease drastically in the not too distant future: see WYNANTS, *België en Nederland op gescheiden wegen?* (see note 6), pp. 65-75.

29. For reviews of the literature see note 6. Important and useful websites are www.kadoc.kuleuven.be/relins/eu/ and www.rhul.ac.uk/Bedford-Centre/history-women-religious/.

30. CLEAR, *Nuns* (see note 26); M.P. MAGRAY, *The Transforming Power of the Nuns: Women, Religion, and Cultural Change in Ireland, 1750-1900*, New York, Oxford University Press, 1998; B. MISNER, *"Highly Respectable and Accomplished Ladies": Catholic Women Religious in America 1790-1850*, New York/London, Garland, 1988 (a comparative study of 8 religious orders established in the US before 1850); G.C. STEWART JR., *Marvels of Charity: History of American Sisters and Nuns*, Huntington, Our Sunday Visitor, 1994; S. HOY, *Good Hearts: Catholic Sisters in Chicago's Past*, Urbana, University of Illinois Press, 2006; M.R. MACGINLEY, *A Dynamic of Hope: Institutes of Women Religious in Australia*, Sydney, Crossing Press, 1996 (from its origins

to 1940); A. O'BRIEN, *God's Willing Workers: Women and Religion in Australia*, Sydney, University of New South Wales Press, 2005 (including a section on the Catholic sisters); R. MEIWES, *Arbeiterinnen des Herrn: katholische Frauenkongregationen im 19. Jahrhundert* (Geschichte und Geschlechter 30), Frankfurt, Campus, 2000 (primarily about Prussia; on this work see also C. MAURER, *Le catholicisme au féminin: l'expansion des congrégations dans l'Allemagne du XIXe siècle*, in: *Histoire, Economie et Société*, 21:1 (2002), pp. 17-28); E. GATZ (ed.), Geschichte *des kirchlichen Lebens in den deutschsprachigen Ländern seit dem Ende des 18. Jahrhunderts, vol. 7: Klöster und Ordensgemeinschaften*, Herder, Freiburg, 2006; P. BRAUN (ed.), *Die Kongregationen in der Schweiz 19. und 20. Jahrhundert* (Helvetica Sacra 8.2), Basel, Schwabe, 1998; B. WALSH, *Roman Catholic Nuns in England and Wales 1800-1937: A Social History*, Dublin, Irish Academic Press, 2002; C.M. MANGION, *Contested Identities: Catholic Women Religious in Nineteenth-century England and Wales*, Manchester, Manchester University Press, 2008; N. LAURIN, D. JUTEAU & L. DUCHESNE, *À la recherche d'un monde oublié. Les communautés religieuses de femmes au Québec de 1900 à 1970*, Montréal, Le Jour, 1991; D. RINK, *Spirited Women: A History of Catholic Sisters in British Columbia*, Vancouver, Sisters Association of Vancouver Archdiocese, 2000. For Canada, see now also a collection of essays by leading scholars: E. SMYTH (ed.), *Changing habits. Women's Religious Orders in Canada*, Montreal, Novalis, 2007. Important forthcoming studies are M.S. THOMPSON, *The Yoke of Grace: American Nuns and Social Change, 1808-1917*, to be published by Oxford University Press; M. DERKS & A. VAN HEIJST, *Voor mensen, om God. De spirituele en sociale betekenis van vrouwelijke religieuzen in Nederland in de 19e en 20e eeuw.*

31. *Cf.* P.J. HARRIGAN, *The 'Histoire de l'éducation' and Canadian Historians*, in: *Historical Studies in Education/Revue d'histoire de l'éducation*, 3:2 (1991), pp. 269-273.

32. H. RIBEIRO DE CASTRO, *Teresa de Saldanha: Um projecto pedagógico inovador no século XIX, uma interrogação para o século XXI*, PhD dissertation, University of Lisbon, 2008. *Cf.* H. RIBEIRO DE CASTRO, *Teresa de Saldanha – um projecto inovador no século XIX; uma interrogação para o século XXI*, in: M. FERNANDES, J.A. GONÇALVES, M. BOLINA, T. SALVADO & T. VITORINO (eds.), *O particular e o global no virar do milénio: cruzar saberes em educação. Actas do 5º congresso da sociedade portuguesa de ciências da educação*, Porto, Edições Colibri/SPCE, 2002, pp. 539-547; H. RIBEIRO DE CASTRO, *The role of feminine civic societies and religious congregations in the history of educational and social change: A Portuguese case*, Paper presented at *The European Conference on Educational Research (ECER) 2008: From Teaching to Learning?*, Göteborg, 11 September, 2008.

33. L.E. GALVÁN LAFARGA & O. LÓPEZ PÉREZ (eds.), *Entre imaginarios y Utopías: Historias de maestras*, México, CIESAS-UNAM-PUEG, 2008. For the contributions see notes 86 and 97.

34. The official title of the conference is *Educating a Catholic Elite. Religious Institutes, Faith, and Gender in Catholic Secondary Education in Europe in the Nineteenth and Twentieth Century.*

35. For her unpublished doctoral dissertation see E.M. SMYTH, *The Lessons of Religion and Science: the Congregation of the Sisters of St. Joseph and St. Joseph's Academy, Toronto, 1854-1911*, University of Toronto, 1990.

36. P. HARRIGAN, *Women Teachers and the Schooling of Girls in France: Recent Historiographical Trends*, in: *French Historical Studies*, 21:4 (1998), p. 598.

37. O'DONOGHUE & POTTS, *Researching the Lives* (see note 4), pp. 469-481. The quotation comes from T. O'DONOGHUE, *Review of C. Trimingham Jack, Growing Good Catholic Girls: Education and Convent Life in Australia (Melbourne: Melbourne University Press, 2003)*, in: *History of Education Quarterly*, 45:3 (2005), p. 493.

38. S. BURLEY, *Silences and Images in an Australian Catholic School History*, in: *History of Education Researcher*, 79 (2007), pp. 2-10. The school monograph is F. GALE (ed.), *Making Space: Women and Education at St Aloysius College 1880-2000*, Adelaide, Wakefield Press, 2000.

39. D. RAFTERY & C. KILBRIDE, *Reading the Image and Hearing the Voice: Using Technologies to Record and Interpret the Role of Catholic Religious Orders in Education and Literacy Formation*, Paper presented at *ISCHE 28: Technologies of the Word. Literacies in the History of Education*, Umeå, Sweden, 16-19 August, 2006.

40. E. SMYTH, *Preserving Habits: Memory within Communities of English Canadian Women Religious*, in: S.A. COOK, L.R. MCLEAN & K. O'ROURKE (eds.), *Framing Our Past: Canadian Women's History in the Twentieth Century*, Montreal and Kingston, McGill-Queen's University Press, 2001, p. 25.

41. M. DERKS, *Modesty and Excellence: Gender and Sports Culture in Dutch Catholic Schooling, 1900-40*, in: *Gender & History*, 20:1 (2008), pp. 9, 22.

42. C. LEI, *"The Science Ball": Poetry as Historical Evidence*, in: *Canadian Catholic Historical Association Historical Studies*, 70 (2004), p. 28.

43. L. VAN ROMPAEY, M. DEPAEPE & F. SIMON, *A Different Kind of Activism: The Position of Catholic Women Teachers in their Union (Belgium, 1950-1965)*, in: *Sens Public. Revue internationale – International webjournal.* Dossier: Les femmes dans l'action militante, syndicale et revendicative de 1945 à nos jours (www.sens-public.org/spip.php?article685); L. VAN ROMPAEY, M. DEPAEPE & F. SIMON, *Las maestras católicas y la prohibición de matrimonio. Bélgica, 1920-1963*, paper presented at the *15th International Congress of the Asociación de Historiadores Latinoamericanistas Europeos* (AHILA), Leiden, 2008, to be published in a volume on women teachers in Belgium and Mexico (L.E. GALVÁN LAFARGA & F. SIMON (eds.), México, CIESAS).

44. R. ROGERS, *Questioning National Models: The History of Women Teachers in a Comparative Perspective*, Paper presented at the *20th International Congress of Historical Sciences - Women's History Revisited: Historiographical Reflections on Women and Gender in a Global Context*, University of New South Wales, Sydney, Australia, 8-9 July, 2005 (available online).

45. ROGERS, *Retrograde or Modern?* (see note 14), pp. 146, 164; R. ROGERS, *Review of M. HEQUET (ed.), L'éducation des filles au temps de George Sand (Arras: Artois Presses université, 1998)*, in: *CLIO, Histoire, Femmes et Sociétés*, 11 (2000) [= *Parler, chanter, lire, écrire*], online.

46. ROGERS, *Review of HEQUET, L'éducation des filles* (see note 45).

47. N. BAUMGARTEN, *Education and Democracy in Frontier St. Louis: The Society of the Sacred Heart*, in: *History of Education Quarterly*, 34 (1994), pp. 171-192. This study is based on the author's unpublished doctoral dissertation: *Immigrants as Democrats: Education in St. Louis before the Civil War*, PhD dissertation, Harvard University, 1993. See also N. BAUMGARTEN, *Catholic Teaching Orders*, in: L. EISENMANN (ed.), *Historical Dictionary of Women's Education in the United States*, Westport, Greenwood Press, 1998, pp. 71-74.

48. M. DUMONT, *Les religieuses sont-elles féministes?*, Montréal, Bellarmin, 1995, p. 70, based on M. DUMONT & N. FAHMY-EID (eds.), *Les couventines: l'éducation des filles au Québec dans les congrégations religieuses enseignantes 1840-1960*, Montréal, Boréal, 1986, pp. 160-166.

49. C. LANGLOIS, *La fabrique des enseignantes. L'Église catholique, les femmes et l'école en France au XIXe siècle*, in: A. CROIX, A. LESPAGNOL & G. PROVOST (eds.), *Église, éducation, Lumières... Histoires culturelles de la France (1500-1830). En l'honneur de Jean Quéniart*, Rennes, Presses universitaires de Rennes, 1999, pp. 163-169.

50. M.J. OATES, *"The Good Sisters": The Work and Position of Catholic Churchwomen in Boston, 1870-1940*, in: R.E. SULLIVAN & J.M. O'TOOLE (eds.), *Catholic Boston. Studies in*

Religion and Community 1870-1970, Boston, Roman Catholic Archbishop of Boston, 1985, pp. 171-200 (largely about teaching orders); J. MCNERGNEY VINYARD, *For Faith and Fortune: The Education of Catholic Immigrants in Detroit, 1805-1925*, Urbana, University of Illinois Press, 1998 (with much attention to the communities of religious sisters who staffed the schools); M. FRIEDRICH, « *Die Schülerinnen werden liebevoll behandelt - im Ganzen herrscht Zucht und Ordnung »: die Tätigkeit der weiblichen Schulorden in Salzburg*, in: BREHMER & SIMON, *Geschichte der Frauenbildung und Mädchenerziehung in Österreich* (see note 9), pp. 108-127; B. MAIERHOFER, *Schulen der Disziplin hinter Klostermauern. Die Frauenschulorden in Graz im 19. und 20. Jahrhundert*, in: BREHMER & SIMON, *Geschichte der Frauenbildung und Mädchenerziehung in Österreich* (see note 9), pp. 141-161; M. GARCÍA GARGALLO, *L'ensenyament de l'església a la ciutat de Barcelona. Directori Estadístic*, PhD dissertation, University of Barcelona, 1999 (available online); M. D'ALLAIRE, *Les communautés religieuses de Montréal, tome 2: Les communautés religieuses et l'éducation à Montréal, 1657-1900*, Montreal, Éditions du Méridien, 2002 (including male religious educators); F.J. O'HAGAN, *The Contribution of the Religious Orders to Education in Glasgow during the Period 1847-1918*, Lampeter, Edwin Mellen Press, 2006.

51. DUMONT, *Les religieuses sont-elles féministes?* (see note 48), pp. 63-92 ('La tradition éducative des religieuses enseignantes'; about Quebec); M. DUMONT, *Le défi des religieuses enseignantes d'aujourd'hui*, in: *Canadian Woman Studies/Les cahiers de la femme*, 7:3 (1986), pp. 51-54 (the situation in Quebec in 1960); M. DESMEULES, *Les communautés religieuses enseignantes*, in: *Saguenayensia* 44:2 (2002), pp. 27-35 (about a region in Quebec); P. WYNANTS, *L'influence des Congrégations en Luxembourg belge (1830-1970)*, in: A. NEUBERG (ed.), *Entre vêpres et maraude: L'enfance en Ardenne de 1850 à 1950*, Bastogne, Musée en Piconrue, 2008, pp. 185-204; W. SCHAFFER, *Schulorden im Rheinland: ein Beitrag zur Geschichte religiöser Genossenschaften im Erzbistum Köln zwischen 1815 und 1875* (Kölner Schriften zu Geschichte und Kultur 13), Köln, DME-Verlag, 1988; A. RAICHE & A.M. BIERMAIER, *They Came to Teach: The Story of Sisters who Taught in Parochial Schools and their Contribution to Elementary Education in Minnesota*, St. Cloud, North Star Press, 1994; T. WALCH, *The Diverse Origins of American Catholic Education: Chicago, Milwaukee, and the Nation* (The Heritage of American Catholicism 28), New York, Garland, 1988; N. KYLE, *Her Natural Destiny: The Education of Women in New South Wales*, Kensington, New South Wales University Press, 1986 (including a discussion of the contribution of women religious to girls' schooling in this Australian state); F. SAEZ ISERN, *Congregaciones religiosas dedicadas a la enseñanza en Mallorca, 1794-1915*, in: *Mayurqa* 21 (1985-1987), pp. 279-288; A. YETANO LAGUNA, *Congregaciones femeninas de enseñanza fundadas en Cataluña en el siglo XIX*, in: J.-R. AYMES (ed.), *École et Église en Espagne et en Amérique latine: Aspects idéologiques et institutionnels. Actes du colloque de Tours (4-6 décembre 1987)* (Études hispaniques 8-9), Tours, Publications de l'Université de Tours, 1988, pp. 297-307; M. PEREIRA DA SILVA ROSSI & G. INÁCIO FILHO, *As congregações Católicas e a disseminação de escolas femininas no Triângulo Mineiro E Alto Paranaíba*, in: *Revista HISTEDBR On-line*, 24 (2006), pp. 79-92 (about the State of Minas Gerais in Brazil). For an important survey dating back to 1983 see M. DUMONT & M.-P. MALOUIN, *Évolution et rôle des congrégations religieuses enseignantes féminines au Québec, 1840-1960*, in: *SHEC Sessions d'étude*, 50 (1983), pp. 201-230.

52. W. HUG, *Mädchenbildung als Auftrag der Frauenorden. Ein geschichtlicher Rückblick*, in: *Katholische Bildung*, 98:9 (1997), pp. 345-354 (about Germany); A. DEL VALLE LÓPEZ, *La actividad educadora institucional: órdenes, congregaciones e institutos eclesiásticos femeninos dedicados a la educación enseñanza*, in: B. BARTOLOMÉ MARTÍNEZ (ed.), *Historia de la acción educadora de la iglesia en España, II: Edad Contemporánea* (Biblioteca de auto-

res cristianos. Series maior 54), Madrid, Biblioteca de Autores Cristianos, 1997, pp. 512-718; V. FAUBELL ZAPATA, *Educación y órdenes y congregaciones religiosas en la España del siglo XX*, in: *Revista de educación*, 1 (2000), pp. 137-200; BAUMGARTEN, *Catholic Teaching Orders* (see note 47), pp. 71-74; T. WALCH, *Parish School: American Catholic Parochial Education from Colonial Times to the Present*, New York, Crossroad, 1996 (including the role of sister-teachers); T. O'DONOGHUE & S. BURLEY, *God's Antipodean Teaching Force: An Historical Exposition on Catholic Teaching Religious in Australia*, in: *Teaching and Teacher Education*, 24 (2008), pp. 180-189 (with a strong emphasis on female religious); D. RAFTERY & S.M. PARKES, *Female Education in Ireland 1700-1900: Minerva or Madonna*, Ontario, London and Dublin, Frank Cass/ Irish Academic Press, 2007 (including the role of Catholic teaching orders); J.P. CONEJEROS MALDONADO, *Iglesia y educación. Las congregaciones religiosas de origen francés y su presencia en la educación. Chile: 1830-1912*, in: *Revista HISTEDBR On-line*, 26 (2007), pp. 25-38. *Cf.* also F. MAYEUR, *L'éducation des filles vue par l'Église catholique au début du XIXe siècle*, in: G. LEDUC (ed.), *L'éducation des femmes en Europe et en Amérique du Nord de la Renaissance à 1848: réalités et représentations* (Collection 'Des idées et des femmes'), Paris, L'Harmattan, 1997, pp. 442-450; JACOBI, *"Entzauberung der Welt"* (see note 7), pp. 171-186 (about Germany).

53. P. FOZ Y FOZ, *Los monasterios de la enseñanza y la educación de la mujer en España e Iberoamérica*, in: M.I. VIFORCOS MARINAS & J. PANIAGUA PÉREZ (eds.), *I Congreso Internacional del Monacato Femenino en España, Portugal y America, 1492-1992*, vol. 1, León, Universidad de León - Servicio de Publicaciones, 1993, pp. 67-84; T.A. O'DONOGHUE, *Come Follow Me and Forsake Temptation: The Recruitment and Retention of Members of Catholic Teaching Orders, 1922-1965*, Bern, Lang, 2004 (about recruitment, retention and the contribution of male and female orders to Catholic education in a large part of the English-speaking world); E. GATZ (ed.), *Geschichte des Kirchlichen Lebens in den deutschsprachigen Ländern seit dem Ende des 18. Jahrhunderts: Die katholische Kirche, vol. 5: Caritas und soziale Dienste*, Freiburg, Herder, 1997 (including information on the evolution of teaching orders in German-language areas).

54. R. GREW & P.J. HARRIGAN, *The Catholic Contribution to Universal Schooling in France, 1850-1906*, in: *The Journal of Modern History*, 57:2 (1985), pp. 230-231.

55. J.-N. LUC, *L'invention du jeune enfant. De la salle d'asile à l'école maternelle*, Paris, Belin, 1997, pp. 258-264, 310-313.

56. For a case study dating back to 1980 see M. DUMONT, *Des garderies au 19e siècle: les salles d'asile des Soeurs Grises à Montréal*, in: N. FAHMY-EID & M. DUMONT, *Maîtresses de maison, maîtresses d'école: femmes, famille et éducation dans l'histoire du Québec* (Études d'Histoire du Québec), Montréal, Boréal Express, 1983, pp. 261-285.

57. R. GREW & P.J. HARRIGAN, *School, State, and Society: The Growth of Elementary Schooling in Nineteenth-Century France – A Quantitative Analysis*, Ann Arbor, University of Michigan Press, 1991 [translation: *L'école primaire en France au 19e siècle: essai d'histoire quantitative* (Civilisations et sociétés 108), Paris, École des hautes études en sciences sociales, 2002]. *Cf.* GREW & HARRIGAN, *The Catholic Contribution to Universal Schooling in France* (see note 54), pp. 211-247.

58. S.A. CURTIS, *Educating the Faithful: Religion, Schooling, and Society in Nineteenth Century France*, DeKalb, Northern Illinois University Press, 2000 [translation: *L'enseignement au temps des congrégations. Le diocèse de Lyon (1801-1905)*, Lyon, Presses universitaires de Lyon, 2003]. *Cf.* S.A. CURTIS, *Supply and Demand: Religious Schooling in Nineteenth-Century France*, in: *History of Education Quarterly*, 39:1 (1999), pp. 51-72.

59. R. ROGERS, *From the Salon to the Schoolroom: Educating Bourgeois Girls in Nineteenth-Century France*, University Park, Pennsylvania State University Press, 2005 [translation: *Les bourgeoises au pensionnat: L'éducation féminine au XIXe siècle*, Rennes, Presses universitaires de Rennes, 2007]; *Cf.* ROGERS, *La sous-maîtresse française au XIXe siècle* (see note 14), pp. 37-60.

60. B. ZYMEK & G. NEGHABIAN (eds.), *Sozialgeschichte und Statistik des Mädchenschulwesens in den deutschen Staaten 1800-1945* (Datenhandbuch zur deutschen Bildungsgeschichte 2.3), Göttingen, Vandenhoeck & Ruprecht, 2005, chapter 9.

61. MEIWES, *Arbeiterinnen des Herrn* (see note 30).

62. M.J. OATES, *Catholic Female Academies on the Frontier*, in: *U.S. Catholic Historian*, 12:4 (1994), pp. 121-136, esp. pp. 132-135.

63. See e.g. P. BYRNE, *A Tradition of Educating Women: The Religious of the Sacred Heart and Higher Education*, in: *U.S. Catholic Historian*, 13:4 (1995), pp. 49-79; M.J. DAIGLER, *Through the Windows: A History of the Work of Higher Education among the Sisters of Mercy of the Americas*, Scranton, University of Scranton Press, 2000. See also some of the institutional histories mentioned in notes 97 and 98.

64. J. HUNTLEY-MAYNARD, *Catholic Post-secondary Education for Women in Quebec: its Beginnings in 1908*, in: *Canadian Catholic Historical Association Historical Studies*, 59 (1992), pp. 37-48; T. SCHIER & C. RUSSETT (eds.), *Catholic Women's Colleges in America*, Baltimore, The Johns Hopkins University Press, 2002; J. HARFORD, *The Movement for the Higher Education of Women in Ireland: Gender Equality or Denominational Rivalry?*, in: *History of Education*, 34:5 (2005), pp. 497-516; J. HARFORD, *An Experiment in the Development of Social Networks for Women: Women's Colleges in Ireland in the Nineteenth Century*, in: *Paedagogica Historica*, 43:3 (2007), pp. 365-381.

65. HUNTLEY-MAYNARD, *Catholic Post-secondary Education for Women in Quebec* (see note 64); HARFORD, *The Movement for the Higher Education of Women in Ireland* (see note 64).

66. HARFORD, *The Movement for the Higher Education of Women in Ireland* (see note 64).

67. T. LANDY, *The Colleges in Context*, in: SCHIER & RUSSETT, *Catholic Women's Colleges* (see note 64), pp. 55-97.

68. DUMONT, *Le défi des religieuses enseignantes d'aujourd'hui* (see note 51), p. 52.

69. E .g. M.-P. MALOUIN, *Les Congrégations féminines et la fondation des écoles normales de filles à Montréal*, in: E. TARDY et al., *Les bâtisseuses de la Cité* (Les Cahiers scientifiques 79), Montréal, ACFAS, 1993, pp. 141-148.

70. T. HAMEL, *Un siècle de formation des maîtres au Québec, 1836-1939* (Les Cahiers du Québec: collection "Psychopédagogie"), LaSalle, Éditions Hurtubise HMH ltée, 1995; T.A. FITZPATRICK, *No Mean Achievement: Scottish Teacher Education 1895-1995*, Glasgow, Burns & Son, 1995; M. VAN ESSEN, *Kwekeling tussen akte en ideaal: De opleiding tot onderwijzer(es) vanaf 1800*, Amsterdam, SUN, 2006.

71. MALOUIN, *Les Congrégations féminines et la fondation des écoles normales de filles* (see note 69); HAMEL, *Un siècle de formation des maîtres au Québec* (see note 70).

72. T. HAMEL, *Les écoles normales au Québec: institutions d'Église ou d'État?*, in: COOLAHAN, ALDRICH & SIMON, *Faiths and Education* (see note 9), pp. 193-215.

73. VAN ESSEN, *Kwekeling tussen akte en ideaal* (see note 70), p. 120. For the failed attempt by Mother Marie du Sacré-Coeur of the *Filles de Notre-Dame* (Adrienne Laroche) to create a training centre for women religious teachers see F. MAYEUR, *Vers un enseignement secondaire catholique des jeunes filles*, in: G. CHOLVY & N.-J. CHALINE (eds.), *L'enseignement catholique en France aux XIXe et XXe siècles. Actes du colloque organisé par la Société d'histoire religieuse de*

la France (Toulouse, 18-20 mars 1994) et de la journée d'étude de l'Association française d'histoire religieuse contemporaine (Paris, 24 septembre 1994) (Histoire religieuse de la France 8), Paris, Cerf, 1995, p. 201.

74. *Cf.* the remarks by B.M. WALL, *"Definite Lines of Influence": Catholic Sisters and Nurse Training Schools, 1890-1920*, in: *Nursing Research*, 50:5 (2001), pp. 314-321.

75. For a case study of training in domestic science see H. VAN SETTEN & E. VAN GERVEN, *Met wapperend habijt: Geschiedenis van het huishoudonderwijs van de Ursulinen van Bergen NH, 1925-1990*, Bergen, Bernardus Smeemanstichting, 1992. For music education *cf.* D.R. ALLISON & H. PLOUFFE, *Convent Schools*, in: *Encyclopedia of Music in Canada* (online). The study by K. TOLLEY, *Music Teachers in the North Carolina Education Market, 1800-1840*, in: *Social Science History*, 32:1 (2008), pp. 75-106, completely ignores the music instruction given in convent academies.

76. See e.g. E. SMYTH, *Educating the Exceptional Child: English-Canadian Women in Religious and Residential Special Education, 1935-1960*, Paper presented at *ISCHE 26: New Education: Genesis and Metamorphoses*, Geneva, 2004 (Ursulines of the Chatham Union); A. VAN DRENTH, *Religious Inspiration and Professionalism in the Care for the 'Feebleminded' in the Netherlands around 1900*, Paper presented at the *Sixth European Social Science History Conference*, Amsterdam, 22-25 March, 2006 (*Filles de la Sagesse*); J. EIJT, *"Daar was je dochter veilig". Vrouwelijke religieuzen en de zorg voor zwakzinnige meisjes, 1924-1955*, in: A. VAN HEIJST & M. DERKS (eds.), *Terra incognita. Historisch onderzoek naar katholicisme en vrouwelijkheid*, Kampen, Kok Agora, 1994, pp. 149-172 (Congregation of the Sisters of the Choorstraat, officially designated as the *Zusters van liefde, Dochters van Maria en Jozef*); J. EIJT, *"Het is hard werken geweest, dag en nacht." De Zusters van de Choorstraat en hun zorg voor zwakzinnige meisjes, 1924-1955*, in: *Brabants Heem* 48:3 (1996), pp. 103-111.

77. E.g. J. EIJT, *Zorgende zusters en hulpeloze zielen. De opvang van verlaten kinderen in 's-Hertogenbosch 1813-1900*, in: J.A.F.M. VAN OUDHEUSDEN, P.H.A.M. ABELS, J.G.M. BIEMANS & A.P.F. WOUTERS (eds.), *Ziel en zaligheid in Noord-Brabant*, Delft, Eburon, 1993, pp. 332-344; P. GOSSAGE, *Les enfants abandonées à Montréal au 19e siècle: la Crèche d'Youville des Soeurs Grises 1820-1871*, in: *Revue d'histoire de l'Amérique française*, 40:4 (1987), pp. 537-559; M. FITZGERALD, *The Perils of "Passion and Poverty": Women Religious and the Care of Single Women in New York City, 1845-1890*, in: *U.S. Catholic Historian*, 10:1-2 (1992) [= special issue *Women Religious: Historical Explorations*], pp. 45-58 (including the care of children from the streets).

78. E.g. B. TITLEY, *Heil Mary: Magdalen Asylums and Moral Regulation in Ireland*, in: *History of Education Review*, 35:2 (2006), pp. 1-15; T. WOLOSCHUK, *A Promise of Redemption: the Soeurs du Bon Pasteur and Delinquent Girls in Winnipeg, 1911-1948*, in: *Manitoba History*, 51 (Feb. 2006), pp. 16-19.

79. For Canada *cf.* E. SMYTH, *"Sisters Shall not Speak of the Defects": Canadian Women Religious and Youth at Risk 1867-1901*, Paper presented at *ISCHE 29: Children and Youth at Risk*, Hamburg, 2007.

80. S. VROMEN, *Hidden Children of the Holocaust. Belgian Nuns and their Daring Rescue of Young Jews from the Nazis*, New York, Oxford University Press, 2008.

81. I. BOURGEOIS, *The Rideau Street Convent School: French-language Private Schooling in Ontario*, in: S.A. COOK, L.R. MCLEAN & K. O'ROURKE (eds.), *Framing Our Past: Canadian Women's History in the Twentieth Century*, Montreal and Kingston, McGill-Queen's University Press, 2001, pp. 178-183, 455-456.

82. F. DEACON, *More than Just a Shoe String and a Prayer: How Women Religious Helped Finance the Nineteenth-Century Social Fabric*, in: *U.S. Catholic Historian*, 14:1 (1996) [= special issue *Beyond the Walls: Women Religious in American Life*], pp. 67-89.

83. RAFTERY & NOWLAN-ROEBUCK, *Convent Schools and National Education in Nineteenth-Century Ireland* (see note 14), pp. 353-365.

84. M.-P. MALOUIN, *Les rapports entre l'école privée et l'école publique: l'académie Marie-Rose au 19e siècle*, in: N. FAHMY-EID & M. DUMONT, *Maîtresses de maison, maîtresses d'école: femmes, famille et éducation dans l'histoire du Québec* (Études d'Histoire du Québec), Montréal, Boréal Express, 1983, pp. 77-91, 381-382; M.-P. MALOUIN, *Ma soeur, à quelle école allez-vous? Deux écoles de filles à la fin du XIXème siècle, Montreal*, Fides, 1985; M. DUMONT & L. CHAMPAGNE, *Le financement des pensionnats de jeunes filles: le modèle de la congrégation des Sœurs de Sainte-Anne, 1850-1950*, in: *Société canadienne d'histoire de l'Église catholique (SCHEC) Sessions d'étude*, 53 (1986), pp. 63-91; L. CHAMPAGNE & M. DUMONT, *Le financement d'un séminaire diocésain: le Séminaire de Sherbrooke, 1915-1950. Comparaison avec le financement des pensionnats de religieuses*, in: *Historical Studies in Education/Revue d'histoire de l'éducation*, 2:2 (1990), pp. 339-351; M.-J. DELORME, *Les rapports entre le pensionnat Sainte-Marie et la commission scolaire de Yamaskaville, 1930-1960*, in: *Historical Studies in Education/Revue d'histoire de l'éducation*, 3:1 (1991), pp. 49-74; DUMONT, *Les religieuses sont-elles féministes?* (see note 48), pp. 93-128.

85. Interview with G. Greer, included in J. BENNETT & R. FORGAN (eds.), *Convent Girls*, London, Virago, 2003 (updated and revised edition of *There's Something about a Convent Girl*, London, Virago, 1991).

86. R. VANDERSTRAETEN & M. PRENEEL, *175 jaar Zusters der Christelijke Scholen Vorselaar (1820-1995)*, Vorselaar-Leuven, Zusters der Christelijke Scholen – KADOC, 1996; M. KEALY, *Dominican Education in Ireland 1820-1930*, Dublin, Irish Academic Press, 2007. Other instances of this category include: R. CHRISTENS, *100 jaar Heilig-Hartinstituut Annuntiaten Heverlee. Geschiedenis van een school en een congregatie*, Leuven, Annuntiaten – KADOC, 1994; L.M.L. VAN RIJCKEVORSEL, *Een wereld apart. Geschiedenis van het Sacré-Coeur in Nederland van 1848 tot heden*, Hilversum, Verloren, 1996 (about 6 boarding schools conducted by the *Société du Sacré-Coeur de Jésus*); J. EIJT, *Van geestelijke moeders en jonge juffrouwen. Zusters in opvoeding en onderwijs*, in: M. VAN DER PLAS (ed.), *Kostschool...een les voor het leven?*, 's-Hertogenbosch, Het Noordbrabants Genootschap, 1991, pp. 55-76 (*Dochters van Maria en Joseph*); E. FRITZER (ed.), *300 Jahre Englische Fräulein in Österreich. Wegbereiterinnen moderner Frauenbildung*, Lienz, E. Fritzer, 2005; G. LOGAN & T. WATSON (eds.), *Soldiers of the Service: Some Early Queensland Educators and their Schools*, Brisbane, History of Queensland Education Society, 1992 (with a chapter on the Sisters of Mercy's system of schools); J.-C. MEYER, *La congrégation de Notre-Dame de la Compassion*, in: CHOLVY & CHALINE, *L'enseignement catholique en France* (see note 73), pp. 131-144; M.R. GERDES, *To Educate and Evangelize: Black Catholic Schools of the Oblate Sisters of Providence (1828-1880)*, in: *U.S. Catholic Historian*, 7:2-3 (1988), pp. 183-199; M. STANLEY, *Women and Education at St. Ann's Academy, Victoria, British Columbia*, online publication (2000): www.pc.gc.ca/dci/rf-ap/ph3/stann/stann_e.asp; H. NORTHEY, *Saint Mary's Convent Schools*, in: B. DICKEY (ed.), *William Shakespeare's Adelaide 1860-1930*, Adelaide, South Australian Association of Professional Historians, 1992; V. TORRES-SEPTIÉN, *Entre Francia y México: las hermanas educadoras de la orden de San José de Lyon*, in: GALVÁN LAFARGA & LÓPEZ PEREZ, *Entre imaginarios y Utopías* (see note 33). Note also an important PhD dissertation which was published as early as in 1984: P. WYNANTS, *Les Sœurs de la Providence de Champion et leurs écoles, 1833-1914*, Namur, Presses Universitaires de Namur, 1984.

87. E.g. Y. SEGERS, C. DUJARDIN, G. KWANTEN, P. QUAGHEBEUR & J. DE MAEYER, *150 Jaar Zusters van het Heilig Hart van Maria van Berlaar. In eenvoud en dienstbaarheid. 1845-1995*, Leuven, Zusters van het Heilig Hart van Maria, Berlaar & KADOC, 1995; R. TIMMERMANS, *Het convent van Betlehem. Een half millennium vrouwelijke spiritualiteit en bedrijvigheid*, Leuven, KADOC, 2000; F. AUMANN et al., *150 jaar Zusters van Liefde te Sint-Truiden*, Sint-Truiden, Psychiatrisch Ziekenhuis Sancta Maria v.z.w. Sint-Truiden, 1991; G. ACKERMANS, *Vereeniging van vrouwen...Franciscanessen van Heythuysen in Nederland (1900-1975)*, Heythuysen, Provincialaat Franciscanessen van Heythuysen, 1994; J. EIJT, *Religieuze vrouwen. Bruid, moeder, zuster. Geschiedenis van twee Nederlandse zustercongregaties, 1820-1940*, Hilversum, Verloren, 1995 (*Zusters van de Choorstraat* in 's-Hertogenbosch and *Zusters Onder de Bogen* in Maastricht); J. EIJT, *Zorgen in Gods naam. Ursulinen van Bergen 1898-1998*, Hilversum, Verloren, 1998; J. EIJT & S. HAUTVAST, *Een missie in de marge. Dochters van Onze Lieve Vrouw van het Heilig Hart in Nederland en Indonesië 1911-2000*, Hilversum, Verloren, 2002; M. MONTEIRO, *Vroomheid in veelvoud. Geschiedenis van de Franciscanessen van Oirschot 1797-1997*, Hilversum, Verloren, 2000; A. VAN DER VEEN & D. VERHOEVEN, *We Agreed to Be Different: Sisters of Charity of Our Lady Mother of Mercy 1960-2000*, Hilversum, Verloren, 2005; E.W. MCGAHAN, *The Sisters of Charity of the Immaculate Conception: A Canadian Case Study*, in: *Canadian Catholic Historical Association Historical Studies*, 61 (1995), pp. 99-133; E. SMYTH, *Congregavit nos in unum Christi amor: The Congregation of the Sisters of St. Joseph, in the Archdiocese of Toronto, 1851-1920*, in: *Ontario History* 84:3 (1992), pp. 225-240; M. STENGLER, *Where to Now? The Story of the Ursuline Sisters of Prelate 1919-2003*, Saskatoon, Saskatchewan, The Ursuline Sisters of Prelate, 2004; M. DANYLEWYCZ, *Taking the Veil: An Alternative to Marriage, Motherhood and Spinsterhood in Quebec, 1840-1920* (The Canadian Social History Series), Toronto, MacClelland & Stewart, 1987 [translation: *Profession: religieuse: un choix pour les Québécoises, 1840-1920*, Montréal, Boréal, 1988] (a case study of the teaching order of the *Sœurs de la Congrégation de Notre-Dame* and the nursing order of the *Soeurs de Miséricorde*); L. ROY, *The Sisters of Saint Ann: A Century of History, 1900-1950*, vol. 2, Lachine, Les éditions Sainte-Anne, 1994; G.-M. OURY, *Les Ursulines de Québec 1639-1953*, Sillery, Septentrion, 1999; M. CANTWELL, *North to Share*, Victoria, The Sisters of Saint Ann, 1992; C. PETERSON & C.A. VAUGHN-ROBERSON, *Women with Vision: The Presentation Sisters of South Dakota, 1880-1985*, Urbana, University of Illinois Press, 1988; C.K. COBURN & M. SMITH, *Spirited Lives: How Nuns Shaped Catholic Culture and American Life, 1836-1920*, Chapel Hill, University of North Carolina Press, 1999 (they use the experiences of one congregation of women religious, the Sisters of St. Joseph of Carondolet, to examine the lives, work, and contributions of Catholic sisters as a whole); A.M. HARRINGTON, *Creating Community: Mary Frances Clarke and Her Companions*, Dubuque, Sisters of Charity BVM, 2004 (Sisters of Charity of the Blessed Virgin Mary); M.S. MCGRATH, *These Women? Women Religious in the History of Australia: the Sisters of Mercy, Parramatta 1888-1988*, Kensington, New South Wales University Press, 1988; S. BURLEY & K. TEAGUE, *Chapel, Cloister & Classroom: Reflections on the Dominican Sisters at North Adelaide*, Adelaide, Lutheran Publishing House, 1993; A. MCLAY, *Women Out of Their Sphere: A History of the Sisters of Mercy in Western Australia*, Northbridge, W.A. Vanguard Press, 1992; A. MCLAY, *Women on the Move: Mercy's Triple Spiral. A History of the Adelaide Sisters of Mercy, Ireland to Argentina 1856-1880 to South Australia 1880*, Adelaide, Sisters of Mercy, 1996; S.E. CASEY, *Held in our Hearts: A Story of the Sisters of Mercy of the Goulburn Congregation*, Braddon, Sisters of Mercy Goulburn Congregation, 2000; J. BOMBARDIER & A.-M. LAPAGE (eds.), *Histoire des soeurs de la Doctrine Chrétienne de Nancy*, 5 vols., Nancy, Doctrine Chrétienne, 1995; A.-M. PUGA, *Histoire de la Congrégation*

du Saint-Nom de Jésus de Toulouse: de 1800 à 1953, Toulouse, Privat, 2006; M.-T. LACROIX, *La vie à Saint-André au XIXème siècle (1796-1914)*, 2 vols., Tournai, ARSA, Religieuses de Saint-André, 2007.

88. *Cf.* the criticism voiced by M.-M. COMPÈRE, *Review of P. Annaert, Les collèges au féminin. Les Ursulines: enseignement et vie consacrée aux XVIIe et XVIIIe siècles (Namur: Vie consacrée, 1992)*, in: *Histoire de l'éducation*, 57 (1993), p. 117.

89. J. DE VIGUERIE, *Avant-Propos*, in: *Les religieuses enseignantes XVI - XX siècles* (see note 19), p. 7.

90. E.g. R. MCGUIRE, *The Grey Sisters in the Red River Settlement, 1844-1870*, in: *Canadian Catholic Historical Association Historical Studies*, 53 (1986), pp. 21-37; M. NORMAN, *Making a Path by Walking. Loretto Pioneers Facing the Challenges of Catholic Education on the North American Frontier*, in: *Canadian Catholic Historical Association Historical Studies*, 65 (1999), pp. 92-106; M.G. COSTIN, *Priceless Spirit: A History of the Sisters of the Holy Cross, 1841-1893*, Notre Dame, University of Notre Dame Press, 1994; R. BRUNO-JOFRÉ, *The Oblate Sisters, A Manitoba Order: Reconstructing Early Years, 1904-1915*, in: R. BRUNO-JOFRÉ (ed.), *Issues in the History of Education in Manitoba*, Lewiston, The Edwin Mellen Press, 1993, pp. 511-567; L.M.A. BOWMAN, *Women's Religious Education: Liberation or Socialization? A Case Study*, in: *Religious Education*, 88:1 (1993), pp. 22-38 (Society of the Holy Child Jesus); M.T. FOALE, *The Josephite Story: The Sisters of St. Joseph: Their Foundation and Early History 1866-1893*, Sydney, St. Joseph's Generalate, 1989; K.A. BROSNAN, *Public Presence, Public Silence: Nuns, Bishops, and the Gendered Space of Early Chicago*, in: *Catholic Historical Review*, 90:3 (2004), pp. 473-496 (Sisters of Mercy in Chicago); D.B. MORROW, *Persons of Color and Religious at the Same Time: The Oblate Sisters of Providence, 1828-1860*, Chapel Hill/London, University of North Carolina Press, 2002; MARQUESA DE RIO MAIOR, *Fundação da Ordem das Terceiras de S. Domingos em Portugal*, Lisboa, Irmãs Dominicanas de Santa Catarina de Sena, 1987. S. O'BRIEN, *"Terra incognita": The Nun in Nineteenth-century England*, in: *Past and Present*, 121 (1988), pp. 110-140, discusses the genesis and early work of three congregations, two of which were involved in teaching (the Society of the Holy Child Jesus and the Sisters of the Cross). Some articles focus on the early educational endeavours of the congregation abroad: see e.g. C. PAISANT, *Les Soeurs de Picpus en Amérique latine: les premières missions d'éducation*, in: *Transversalités. Revue de l'Institut catholique de Paris*, 71 (1999), pp. 205-228.

91. B. CONDON, *A Church in Entropy: Catholic Adelaide, 1868-1873*, in: *Historical Studies in Education/Revue d'histoire de l'éducation*, 6:3 (1994), pp. 115-137 [= *History of Education Review*, 23:3 (1994), p. 115-137].

92. S. ROSS, *Faithful Companions of Jesus in the Field of Education in Brandon, Manitoba, 1883-1895*, in: *Canadian Catholic Historical Association Historical Studies*, 71 (2005), pp. 79-93.

93. M. LUIRARD, *Les Dames du Sacré-Cœur*, in: J. LALOUETTE & J-P. MACHELON (eds.*), Les Congrégations hors-la-loi? Autour de la loi du 1er juillet 1901*, Paris, Cerf, 2002, pp. 257-270; J.F. STONE, *L'Application de la loi dans l'Aveyron: les Soeurs de Saint-Joseph*, in: LALOUETTE & MACHELON, *Les Congrégations hors-la-loi?*, pp. 271-289; Y. LE GOFF, *Les Répercussions des laïcisations sur les activités des Soeurs de Saint-Joseph de Cluny*, in: *Archives de l'Église de France. Bulletin de l'Association des archivistes de l'Église de France*, 57 (2002), pp. 11-15; M. PÉRON, *Répercussions de la législation scolaire française (fin XIXe siècle début XXe siècle) sur la vie d'une congrégation bretonne: L'Immaculée*, in: *Archives de l'Église de France*, 56 (2001), pp. 15-22 & 57 (2001), pp. 13-24 (*Conception de Saint-Méen le Grand*); L. BOUILLÉ, *Séparation de l'Église et de l'État. Les Ursulines de Château-Gontier*, in: *L'Oribus*, 56 (2002), pp. 3-20; G. COURIAUD, *La*

Présentation de Marie sous la Troisième République, in: B. WACHÉ (ed.), *L'histoire des croyants. Mémoire vivante des hommes. Mélanges Charles Molette*, vol. 2, Abbeville, Paillart, 1989, pp. 719-732. For more general studies on the effects of the secularization of the educational system in France in the late 19th and early 20th centuries see S.A. CURTIS, *Lay Habits: Religious Teachers and the Secularization Crisis of 1901-1904*, in: *French History*, 9:4 (1995), pp. 478-498; S.A. CURTIS, *Persécution et résistance, les congrégations enseignantes face à la loi sur les associations de 1901*, in: *Revue d'histoire de l'Église de France*, 88:1 (2002), pp. 175-195; G. SICARD, *L'offensive de laïcisation de 1870-1871*, in: CHOLVY & CHALINE, *L'enseignement catholique en France* (see note 73), pp. 35-46; LALOUETTE & MACHELON, *Les Congrégations hors-la-loi?* (see this note above); C. SORREL, *La République contre les Congrégations: Histoire d'une passion française (1899-1914)*, Paris, Cerf, 2003; A. LANFREY, *Sécularisation, séparation et guerre scolaire. Les catholiques français et l'école (1901-1914)*, Paris, Cerf, 2003; Anon., *Les congrégations religieuses et la société française d'un siècle à l'autre. Actes du colloque des 17-18 octobre 2003*, Paris, Don Bosco, 2004; P. CABANEL & J.-D. DURAND (eds.), *Le grand exil des congrégations religieuses françaises 1901-1914*, Paris, Cerf, 2005.

94. J. JACOBI, *Schoolmarm, Volkserzieher, Kantor und Schulschwester: German Teachers among German Immigrants during the Second Half of the Nineteenth Century*, in: H. GEITZ et al. (eds.), *German Influences on Education in the United States of America to 1917*, Washington/Cambridge, German Historical Institute/Cambridge University Press, 1995, pp. 115-128; P. BRAUN, *Lehrschwestern und Schulbrüder im Ablauf des Kulturkampfes in der Schweiz (1866-1884)*, in: *Rottenburger Jahrbuch für Kirchengeschichte*, 15 (1996), pp. 115-126; A. OSTROWITZKI, *Höhere Mädchenbildung bei den "Benediktinerinnen von der Ewigen Anbetung" in Bonn. Ein konfessioneller Streitfall im Vorfeld des Kulturkampfes*, in: *Studien und Mitteilungen zur Geschichte des Benediktiner Ordens und seiner Zweige*, 113 (2002), pp. 501-513.

95. L.M. TAGAGE, *Onderwijscongregaties en vrijheid van vereniging. Een aspect van de schoolstrijd in Limburg, 1857-1859*, in: *Maaslands melange. Opstellen over Limburgs verleden. Dr. P.J.H. Ubachs aangeboden bij gelegenheid van zijn 65ste verjaardag* (Werken uitgegeven door het Limburgs Geschied- en Oudheidkundig Genootschap 14), Maastricht, Limburgs Geschied- en Oudheidkundig Genootschap, 1990, pp. 290-303 (*Liefdezusters van de H. Carolus Borromeus*).

96. M.-L. CRONE, *Die Auflösung katholischer Ordensschulen für Mädchen im Bistum Limburg während der Nationalsozialistischen Herrschaft*, in: *Archiv für mittelrheinische Kirchengeschichte*, 42 (1990), pp. 237-252; A. KLARE, *Die Deutschen Heimschulen 1941-1945. Zur Gleichschaltung und Verstaatlichung kirchlicher, privater und stiftlicher Internatschulen im Nationalsozialismus*, in: *Jahrbuch für Historische Bildungsforschung*, 9 (2003), pp. 50-52 (*Stiftsschule Heiligengrabe*).

97. E.g. O. VAN DAMME, *Van Spinhuis tot Hogeschool, 1877-1998. 120 jaar normaalschool Gijzegem*, n.p., n.e., 2002; P. WYNANTS, *Chronique d'histoire scolaire, 4: Quenast, une école congréganiste au pays des carrières (1874-1914)*, in: *Revue d'histoire religieuse du Brabant wallon*, 19:3 (2005), pp. 175-187; F. DE WAELE, *Van Deugdsaeme Dogters en Vroome Meyskens. Pensionaatsopvoeding bij de Zusters van Liefde te Beerlegem 1823-1965*, Beerlegem, Mariaheem, 1985; H.J. OLDENHOF, *Van Normaalschool Steenwijkerwold naar Pabo Zwolle*, Zwolle, Pabo, 1987 (*Zusters van De Voorzienigheid*); N. VAN DER HEIJDEN-ROGIER, *Regina Coeli: Klooster en meisjespensionaat in Vught 1903-1971*, Nijmegen, Valkhof Pers, 2002; J. BROEKHUIZEN (ed.), *Van mystiek naar methode: de "nonnen van Vught"*, Vught, Taleninstituut Regina Coeli, 2003; R. CADOTTE & N. COLETTE, *L'école Notre-Dame-de-l'Assomption, Louis-Jolliet,* Montréal, Commission scolaire de Montréal, 2001; SMYTH, *Loretto Academy Niagara* (see note 15), pp. 25-42; SŒUR LOUISE-MARGUERITE (ed.), *Un héritage: réminiscences du Couvent de la rue*

Rideau et du Collège Bruyère – A Light Rekindled: Reminiscences of Rideau Street Convent and Bruyère College, Ottawa, Sœurs de la Charité d'Ottawa, 1988; J.D. CAMERON, *For the People: A History of St. Francis Xavier University*, Montreal/Kingston, McGill-Queen's Press, 1996; T. CORCORAN, *Mount Saint Vincent University: A Vision Unfolding, 1873-1988*, Lanham, University Press of America, 1999 (primarily about the role of the Sisters of Charity in the institution's development); S. LESSARD, *"The Luxury of Order"*, in: *House Beautiful*, Dec. 1995, pp. 16-124 (on the convent of the Sacred Heart school in Noroton, Conn.); J. SAFIAN, *Educating the Heart and Mind: A History of Marymount School, 1926-2001*, New York, Marymount School, 2002 (Sacred Heart of Mary); Anon., *Festschrift des St.-Franziskus-Gymnasiums in Olpe. Aus Anlaß der Wiedereröffnung vor 100 Jahren*, Olpe, St.-Franziskus-Gymnasium, 1993; M. THIATILDE (ed.), *Das Josefshaus in Vreden. 1911 - 2001. 90 Jahre Schwestern Unserer Lieben Frau in Vreden. Erinnerungen und Berichte (*Beiträge des Heimatvereins Vreden zur Landes- und Volkskunde 59), Vreden, Heimatverein Vreden, 2001; R. WILLIAMS, *From Isolation to Integration: St Mary's Hall, University of Melbourne, 1918-1968*, in: *History of Education Review*, 27:1 (1998), pp. 19-32; H. RIBEIRO DE CASTRO, *A Portuguese School in the 19th Century: Reconstructing Life from Dead Documents*, Paper presented at the *European Conference on Educational Research*, University of Hamburg, 17-20 September, 2003, available on Educati*on-line*; H. RIBEIRO DE CASTRO, *Difusão da Cultura e Promoção da Vida: uma escola no centro de um bairro pobre na Lisboa do século XIX*, in: *Actas do V Congresso Luso-Brasileiro de História da Educação*, Évora, Universidade de Évora, forthcoming (Dominican Sisters of Santa Catarina de Sena; Lisbon); M. LLUÏSA CANUT & J. LUIS AMORÓS, *Maestras y libros (1850-1912): La primera Normal femenina de Baleares*, Palma/Mao, Universitat de les Illes Balears/Institut Menorquí d'Estudis, 2000; I. DE AZCÁRATE RISTORI, *El Monasterio de la Enseñanza de Barcelona, 1645-1876*, Barcelona, PPU, 1993 (*Compañía de María Nuestra Señora*); P. FOZ Y FOZ, *El convento de la enseñanza de México: ambivalencias de una joya de arte colonial*, Bogotá, CELAM, 1990 (*Compañía de María*); M. DEL PILAR GUTIÉRREZ LORENZO, *La escuela para señoritas fundada por las hermanas de la Caridad en 1861: el primer plantel de maestras en Jalisco*, in: GALVÁN LAFARGA & LÓPEZ PEREZ, *Entre imaginarios y Utopías* (see note 33); P. FOZ Y FOZ, *Mujer y educación en Colombia Siglos XVI-XIX. Portaciones del Colegio de La Enseñanza, 1783-1900*, Santa fe de Bogotá, Academia Colombiana de Historia, 1997 (*Compañía de María*); M. SOCHIN, *"Du Mäglein höre!" Das Höhere Töchterinstitut St. Elisabeth 1935-1994* (Religion - Politik - Gesellschaft in der Schweiz 48), Fribourg, Academic Press, 2007 (school in the Principality of Liechtenstein led by the *Kongregation Anbeterinnen des Blutes Christi*); A. HARRINGTON & P. MOYLAN (eds.), *Mundelin Voices: The Women's College Experience 1930-1991*, Chicago, Loyola, 2001 (college for higher education of the Presentation of the Blessed Virgin Mary in Chicago); C. D'AINVAL, *Le couvent des Oiseaux. Ces jeunes filles de bonne famille*, Paris, Perrin, 1991.

98. M. HAYES, *The Founding Years of Trinity College Washington, D.C.: A Case Study in Christian Feminism*, in: *U.S. Catholic Historian*, 10:1-2 (1992) [= special issue *Women Religious: Historical Explorations*], pp. 79-86 (college for the higher education of women run by the *Sœurs de Notre-Dame de Namur*); E.M. SMYTH, *The Culture of Catholic Women's Colleges at the University of Toronto 1911-1925*, in: *Canadian Catholic Historical Association Historical Studies*, 70 (2004), pp. 111-130 (the Sisters of St Joseph and the Loretto Sisters).

99. J. HAMILTON, *The Nunnery as Menace: The Burning of the Charlestown Convent 1834*, in: *U.S. Catholic Historian*, 14:1 (1996) [= special issue *Beyond the Walls: Women Religious in American Life*], pp. 35-65; P. WYNANTS, *Une école congréganiste dans la lutte scolaire: les soeurs de la Providence à Cuesmes, 1859-1895*, in: *Annales du Cercle archéologique de Mons*, 76 (1994), pp. 367-383.

100. S. HOY, *No Color Line at Loretto Academy: Catholic Sisters and African Americans on Chicago's South Side*, in: *Journal of Women's History*, 14:1 (2002), pp. 8-33 (about the 1950s & 1960s) (reprinted in HOY, *Good Hearts* (see note 30)); M. LINEHAN, *"Nazareth College Leads the Way": Catholicism, Democracy, and Racial Justice at a Southern College, 1920-1955*, in: *U.S. Catholic Historian*, 19:1 (2001), pp. 65-77. For other school histories focusing on a limited period see: D. GATTI JÚNIOR & L.H.M. DE M. OLIVEIRA, *Colégio Santa Teresa: um projeto Scalabriniano (1939-1942)*, in: *Revista HISTEDBR On-line*, 9 (March 2003) (Missionary Sisters of St. Charles Borromeo Scalabrinian in Minas Gerais in Brazil); D. GATTI JÚNIOR & L.H.M. DE M. OLIVEIRA, *O Projeto Scalabriniano de Instrução Escolar: o Colégio Santa Teresa de Ituiutaba (1939-1942)*, in: *II Congresso de Pesquisa e Ensino em História da Educação em Minas Gerais, 2004, Uberlândia/MG. Anais do II Congresso de Pesquisa e Ensino em História da Educação em Minas Gerais*, vol. 1, Uberlândia, Editora da Universidade Federal de Uberlândia, 2003, pp. 815-825; M. BRASIL SILVA & G. INÁCIO FILHO, *O Curso Normal Do Colégio Sagrado Coração De Jesus – 1931-1947, processo pedagógico*, in: *Revista HISTEDBR On-line*, 15 (September 2004) (Sisters of the Sacred Heart of Maria, Araguari, Brazil); M.J. SILVIA BASTOS, *Mulheres na sala de aula*, in: *Revista HISTEDBR On-line*, 21 (March 2006), pp. 15-25 (Normal School *Nossa Senhora do Carmo* in Viçosa in Brazil, between 1917-1930); L. DE LIMA MANÇUR LINS, *Um olhar sobre o Colégio Santíssimo Sacramento (1940 – 1960) – Alguns aspectos da educação feminina em Alagoinhas-BA*, in: *Revista HISTEDBR On-line*, 21 (March 2006) (Brazil); G. FERREIRA MELO & G. INÁCIO FILHO, *Colégio Nossa Senhora Das Dores - Uberaba-Mg (1940-1966); Educação feminina*, in: *Revista HISTEDBR On-line*, 15 (September 2004) (school of the Dominican Sisters, Brazil).

101. F. SIMON, *De produktie van schoolgedenkboeken (1977-1982). Weinig gelegenheid tot gejubel*, in: *Persoon en gemeenschap*, 35:7 (1982-1983), pp. 314-321. *Cf.* S. DELAMONT, *The Beech-covered Hillside: Self-presentation in the Histories of the Girls' Schools*, in: G. WALFORD (ed.), *The Private Schooling of Girls. Past and Present*, London, Woburn Press, 1993, pp. 79-100.

102. M-P. MALOUIN, *Review of* C. AINSLEY, *Eulalie Durocher (Laval: Méridien, 1993) ...*, in: *SCHEC Études d'histoire religieuse*, 60 (1994), p. 141.

103. P. WYNANTS, *Comment écrire l'histoire d'une communauté de religieuses enseignantes (XIX-XXe siècle)*, in: *Leodium* 1987, pp. 1-36; P. WYNANTS, *Pour écrire l'histoire d'un établissement d'enseignement congréganiste: orientations de recherche, sources et méthodes (XIXe - XXe siècles)*, in: *Insediamenti e iniziative Salesiane dopo Don Bosco. Saggi di storiografia* (Istituto Storico Salesiano Roma - Studi 9), Roma, LAS, 1996, pp. 17-62; P. WYNANTS, *Per la storia di un'istituzione insegnante religiosa: orientamenti di recerca, fonti e metodi (XIX - XX secolo)*, in: *Richerche Storiche Salesiane*, 15:1 (1996), pp. 7-54; P. WYNANTS, *Writing the History of a Religious Teaching Institute: Guidelines for Research, Sources and Methods (19th and 20th centuries)*, in: *Journal of Salesian Studies*, 8 (1998), pp. 91-142.

104. WYNANTS, *België en Nederland op gescheiden wegen?* (see note 6), p. 66.

105. G. LAPERRIÈRE, *Comment écrit-on l'histoire d'une communauté? Note critique*, in: *SCHEC Études d'histoire religieuse*, 71 (2005), p. 109.

106. LAPERRIÈRE, *Comment écrit-on l'histoire d'une communauté?* (see note 105), pp. 109-110.

107. A. VIÑAO, *Review of* A. COSTA RICO, *Historia da educación e da cultura en Galicia (séculos IV-XX) (Vigo: Edicións Xerais de Galicia, 2004)*, in: *Paedagogica Historica*, 42:3 (2006), pp. 448-449.

108. R. BRUNO-JOFRE, *Lifting the Veil: The Founding of the Missionary Oblate Sisters of the Sacred Heart and Mary Immaculate in Manitoba*, in: *Historical Studies in Education/Revue*

d'histoire de l'éducation, 9:1 (1997), pp. 1-20. See also R. BRUNO-JOFRÉ, *The Missionary Oblate Sisters: Vision and Mission*, Montreal/Kingston, McGill-Queen's Press, 2005.

109. M.S. THOMPSON, *Review of Ann M.* HARRINGTON, *Creating Community: Mary Frances Clarke and Her Companions (Dubuque: Sisters of Charity - BVM, 2004)*, in: *The Catholic Historical Review*, 92:4 (2006), pp. 695-697. For a plea to adopt a critical perspective in the study of the foundation of religious orders see D. MCLAUGHLIN, *The Founding of the Irish Christian Brothers: Navigating the Realities through the Myths*, in: *Australian Ejournal of Theology* August 2005, Issue 5.

110. E.M. SMYTH & L.F. WICKS (eds.), *Wisdom Raises Her Voice: The Sisters of St. Joseph of Toronto Celebrate 150 Years: An Oral History*, Toronto, Transcontinental Press, 2001.

111. C. LEI, *The Material Culture of the Loretto School for Girls in Hamilton, Ontario, 1865-1971*, in: *Canadian Catholic Historical Association Historical Studies*, 66 (2000), pp. 92-113.

112. C. TRIMINGHAM JACK, *Growing Good Catholic Girls: Education and Convent Life in Australia*, Melbourne, Melbourne University Press, 2003.

113. The 'lay sisters' undertook domestic work and are to be distinguished from the 'choir nuns' who did the teaching and administrative duties; see also C. TRIMINGHAM JACK, *The Lay Sister in Educational History and Memory*, in: *History of Education*, 29:3 (2000), pp. 181-194.

114. MALOUIN, *Ma soeur, à quelle école allez-vous?* (see note 84).

115. MALOUIN, *Ma soeur, à quelle école allez-vous?* (see note 84), p. 67. For a summary of this aspect of the study see also MALOUIN, *Les rapports entre l'école privée et l'école publique* (see note 84).

116. GALE, *Making Space* (see note 38).

117. ROGERS, *From the Salon to the Schoolroom* (see note 59), p. 151.

118. ROGERS, *From the Salon to the Schoolroom* (see note 59), pp. 151-152.

119. MCNERGNEY VINYARD, *For Faith and Fortune* (see note 50).

120. WALCH, *The Diverse Origins of American Catholic Education* (see note 51), p. 195.

121. C. MOLETTE, *Conclusions*, in: *Les religieuses enseignantes XVI - XX siècles* (see note 19), p. 161.

122. L.M.A. BOWMAN, *The History of Women, Religion and Education: A Methodological Approach*, in: *Toronto Journal of Theology*, 11:2 (1995), pp. 201-216.

123. BOWMAN, *Women's Religious Education* (see note 90), pp. 22-38; R. MCDOUGALL, *Cornelia Connelly's Innovations in Female Education, 1846-1864. Revolutionizing the School Curriculum for Girls*, Lewiston, Edwin Mellen Press, 2008.

124. C. TRIMINGHAM JACK, *A Moulding Haven? Competing Educational Discourses in an Australian Preparatory School of the Society of the Sacred Heart, 1944-65*, in: *Historical Studies in Education/Revue d'histoire de l'éducation*, 10:1-2 (1998), pp. 116-39.

125. C. SYMES, Paper presented at the *26th Annual Conference of the Australian & New Zealand History of Education Society*, Brisbane, 1996 (unpublished).

126. C. TRIMINGHAM JACK, *Sacred Symbols, School Ideology and the Construction of Subjectivity*, in: *Paedagogica Historica*, 34:3 (1998), pp. 771-794.

127. C. TRIMINGHAM JACK, *Reproducing an English Sensibility: Landscape and Schooling in the Southern Highlands of New South Wales, 1944-1965*, in: *History of Education Review*, 31:2 (2002), pp. 1-15.

128. For these approaches, which are currently very much in vogue in the history of education, see e.g. C. BURKE (ed.), *Containing the School Child: Architectures and Pedagogies*, Special issue of *Paedagogica Historica*, 41:4-5 (2005); M.L. ALBINO BENCOSTTA (ed.), *História da*

Educação, Arquitetura e Espaço Escolar, São Paulo, Cortez Editora, 2005; M. LAWN & I. GROSVENOR (eds.), *Materialities of Schooling. Design, Technology, Objects, Routines*, Oxford, Symposium Books, 2005; A. ESCOLANO (ed.*), La cultura material de la escuela. En el centenario de la Junta para la Ampliación de Estudios, 1907-2007*, Berlanga de Duero, Soria CEINCE, 2007; A. VAN GORP (ed.), *Materiële schoolcultuur. Over artefacten als bron in de onderwijsgeschiedenis*, special issue of *Jaarboek voor de geschiedenis van opvoeding en onderwijs*, 2008. In July 2007 a symposium was held in Hamburg on the 'spatial turn' and the history of education.

129. For a study of the architecture of 18th century convent schools see L. LECOMTE, *Architecture para-conventuelle: les pensionnats de l'ordre de la Visitation au XVIIIe siècle*, Paper presented at the *5me Rencontre d'architecture européenne: Bâtiments Publiques II (Les écoles, les universités et les bâtiments des institutions sociales)*, Utrecht, 2008.

130. For the concept of 'education markets' in the history of education see N. BEADIE, *Toward a History of Education Markets in the United States. An Introduction*, in: *Social Science History*, 32:1 (2008), pp. 47-73.

131. MALOUIN, *Les rapports entre l'école privée et l'école publique* (see note 115), p. 91.

132. O'HAGAN, *The Contribution of the Religious Orders* (see note 50), p. 113.

133. M. DEPAEPE et al., *Orde in vooruitgang: Alledaags handelen in de Belgische lagere school (1880-1970)* (Studia Paedagogica 25), Leuven, Universitaire Pers, 1999, p. 48 [translation: *Order in Progress: Everyday Educational Practice in Primary Schools, Belgium, 1880-1970* (Studia paedagogica 29), Leuven, Leuven University Press, 2000, p. 45].

134. For this important research field in the history of education see e.g. P. GORDON & D. LAWTON, *Curriculum Change in the Nineteenth and Twentieth Centuries*, London, Hodder & Stoughton, 1978; I. GOODSON (ed.), *International Perspectives in Curriculum History*, London, Routledge, 1988; L.M. BURLBAW & S.L. FIELD (eds.), *Explorations in Curriculum History Research*, Greenwich, CT: Information Age Publishing, 2005.

135. A. DUFOUR, *Les manuels de "Connaissances scientifiques usuelles" des Soeurs de Sainte-Anne, 1923-1956*, in: M. LEBRUN (ed.), *Le manuel scolaire d'ici et d'ailleurs, d'hier à demain*, Québec, Presses de l'université du Québec, 2007.

136. M. LEBRUN, *Un florilège moralisateur et nationaliste: le canon des études littéraires selon les manuels des communautés religieuses québécoises (1900-1950)*, in: *SCHEC Études d'histoire religieuse*, 71 (2005), pp. 33-50.

137. E. DRIVER, *Culinary Landmarks. A Bibliography of Canadian Cookbooks, 1825-1949*, Toronto, University of Toronto Press, 2008, esp. pp. xxiv, 78.

138. M. DUMONT, *Girls' Schooling in Quebec: 1639-1960 (Historical Booklet No. 49), Ottawa*, Canadian Historical Association, 1990, p. 15.

139. STANLEY, *Women and Education at St. Ann's Academy* (see note 86).

140. See for example the important study on the history of secondary education in public high schools in the US: J.L. RURY, *Education and Women's Work. Female Schooling and the Division of Labor in Urban America, 1870-1930*, Albany, State University of New York Press, 1991.

141. E.M. BREWER, *Nuns and the Education of American Catholic Women, 1860-1920*, Chicago, Loyola University Press, 1987 (the schools were founded by 4 communities of women religious).

142. A. GAGNON, *The Pensionnat Assomption: Religious Nationalism in a Franco-Albertan Boarding School for Girls, 1926-1960*, in: *Historical Studies in Education/Revue d'histoire de l'éducation*, 1:1 (1989), pp. 95-117.

143. M. DE SAINT MARTIN, *Une "bonne" éducation: Notre-Dame des Oiseaux à Sèvres*, in: *Ethnologie française*, 20:1 (1990), pp. 62-70.

144. S. BURLEY, *Resurrecting the Religious Experiences of Catholic Girls' Schooling in South Australia in the 1920s*, in: *Education Research and Perspectives*, 28:1 (2001), pp. 25-44.

145. DERKS, *Modesty and Excellence* (see note 41), p. 17. Ingrid Querton demonstrated how the teacher training in a Belgian school conducted by sisters in the 19th century involved a complete personality formation based on religion: see I. QUERTON, *La formation et la vie spirituelle des institutrices à l'école normale de l'Enfant Jésus (Nivelles) aux XIXe siècle*, in: *Revue d'histoire religieuse du Brabant wallon*, 2 (1988), pp. 288-289; I. QUERTON, *La préparation des institutrices à l'Institut de l'Enfant-Jésus (Nivelles) au 19e siècle: une formation totale de la personnalité*, in: L. COURTOIS & J. PIROTTE (eds.), *Foi, gestes et institutions religieuses aux 19e et 20e siècles* (Collection Cerfaux-Lefort 9), Louvain-la-Neuve, UCL Centre d'histoire des religions, 1991, pp. 109-115. On this topic, *cf.* also R. ROGERS, *La place de la religion dans la formation des enseignantes religieuses et laïques en France avant 1880*, Paper presented at the *Journée d'études 'Religion, fait religieux et laïcité dans la formation des enseignants (XVIe-XXe siècles)'*, Lille, 14 November, 2008.

146. DERKS, *Modesty and Excellence* (see note 41), p. 17.

147. E. SMYTH, *"A Noble Proof of Excellence": The Culture and Curriculum of a Nineteenth-Century Ontario Convent Academy*, in: R. HEAP & A. PRENTICE (eds.), *Gender and Education in Ontario: An Historical Reader*, Toronto, Canadian Scholars' Press, 1991, pp. 269-290; E. SMYTH, *"Developing the Powers of the Youthful Mind": The Evolution of Education for Young Women at St. Joseph's Academy, Toronto, 1854-1911*, in: *Canadian Catholic Historical Association Historical Studies*, 60 (1993-1994), pp. 103-125.

148. LEI, *The Material Culture of the Loretto School for Girls* (see note 111), pp. 92-113; LEI, *"The Science Ball"* (see note 42), pp. 9-28.

149. BOWMAN, *Women's Religious Education* (see note 90), pp. 22-38.

150. M. THEOBALD, *"Mere Accomplishments?" Melbourne's Early Ladies' Schools Reconsidered*, in: *History of Education Review*, 13 (1984), pp. 15-28, esp. p. 16 (reprinted in: PRENTICE & THEOBALD, *Women who Taught* (see note 22), pp. 71-91).

151. M. DE VROEDE, *The Catholic Boarding Schools for Girls in Belgium before the First World War*, in: H. KANZ (ed.), *Bildungsgeschichte als Sozialgeschichte. Festschrift zum 60. Geburtstag von Franz Pöggeler* (Erziehungsphilosophie 8), Frankfurt am Main, Peter Lang, 1986, pp. 313-337.

152. R. ROGERS, *Les demoiselles de la Légion d'honneur*, Paris, Plon, 1992; R. ROGERS, *Reconsidering the Role of Religious Orders in Modern French Women's Education*, in: *Vitae Scholasticae*, 10:1-2 (1991), pp. 43-51; ROGERS, *Retrograde or modern?* (see note 14), pp. 146, 149, 160-164.

153. A. BARBARO, *Recovering the Origins of Convent Education in Australia*, in: *Journal of the Australian Catholic Historical Society*, 24 (2003), pp. 45-56.

154. C. MATTINGLY, *Uncovering Forgotten Habits: Anti-Catholic Rhetoric and Nineteenth-Century American Women's Literacy*, in: *College Composition and Communication*, 58:2 (2006), pp. 160-181. For the Protestant rhetoric surrounding the dangers of non-Catholic girls attending convent schools in 19th century England see R. KOLLAR, *Foreign and Catholic: A Plea to Protestant Parents on the Dangers of Convent Education in Victorian England*, in: *History of Education*, 31:4 (2002), pp. 335-350.

155. OATES, *Catholic Female Academies* (see note 62), pp. 123-125.

156. OATES, *Catholic Female Academies* (see note 62), p. 125.

157. WALCH, *The Diverse Origins of American Catholic Education* (see note 51).

158. W.J. GALUSH, *What Should Janek Learn? Staffing and Curriculum in Polish-American Parochial Schools, 1870-1940*, in: *History of Education Quarterly*, 40:4 (2000), pp. 395-417.

159. K. TOLLEY, *"Many Years before the Mayflower": Catholic Academies and the Development of Parish High Schools in the United States, 1727-1925*, in: N. BEADIE & K. TOLLEY (eds.), *Chartered Schools: Two Hundred Years of Independent Academies in the United States, 1727-1925*, New York, RoutledgeFalmer, 2002, p. 322.

160. C.O. WHITE, *Maintaining Anglo-Celtic Cultural Hegemony in Saskatchewan: Rev. E.H. Oliver, Provincial Educational Policy, and the German Catholics*, in: *Historical Studies in Education/Revue d'histoire de l'éducation*, 6:2 (1994), pp. 253-279.

161. For the latter *cf.* S. BURLEY, *Voices, Cultures and Pedagogies in Catholic Convent Classrooms: South Australia, 1880-2000*, Paper presented at *ISCHE 26: New Education: Genesis and Metamorphoses*, Geneva, 2004.

162. W.S. LONGSTREET & H.G. SHANE, *Curriculum for a New Millennium*, Boston, Allyn and Bacon, 1993, p. 46.

163. COBURN & SMITH, *Spirited Lives* (see note 87), p. 167.

164. B.B. SIGMUND, *Sanctuary or prison? Review of V.V. Harrison, Changing Habits: A Memoir of the Society of the Sacred Heart (New York: Doubleday, 1988)*, in: *The New York Times*, May 7, 1989.

165. S. BURLEY, *Past Principals: "The Public Pervasive Presence of Powerful Women in the Church" in South Australia, 1880-1925*, in: J. COOLAHAN, R. ALDRICH & F. SIMON (eds.), *Faiths and Education: Historical and Comparative Perspectives* (*Paedagogica Historica* Supplementary Series 5), Gent, CSHP, 1999, p. 347.

166. ROGERS, *From the Salon to the Schoolroom* (see note 59), p. 159.

167. LEI, *"The Science Ball"* (see note 42), pp. 9-28.

168. S. ANDREW, *Gender and Nationalism: Acadians, Québécois, and Irish in New Brunswick Nineteenth-Century Colleges and Convent Schools, 1854-1888*, in: *Canadian Catholic Historical Association Historical Studies*, 68 (2002), pp. 7-23.

169. ANDREW, *Gender and Nationalism* (see note 168), p. 23.

170. DERKS, *Modesty and Excellence* (see note 41), pp. 8-26.

171. H. SILVER, *Knowing and not Knowing in the History of Education*, in: *History of Education*, 21:1 (1992), p. 105; M. DEPAEPE & F. SIMON, *Is there any Place for the History of "Education" in the "History of Education"? A Plea for the History of Everyday Educational Reality in- and outside Schools*, in: *Paedagogica Historica*, 31:1 (1995), pp. 9-16; I. GROSVENOR, M. LAWN & K. ROUSMANIERE (eds.), *Silences and Images: the Social History of the Classroom*, New York, Peter Lang, 1999.

172. E.g. E. GRUBER, *Erziehungs- und Bildungsarbeit der Franziskanerinnen von Sießen in der Zeit von 1854 bis 1940*, in: *Rottenburger Jahrbuch für Kirchengeschichte*, 14 (1995), pp. 153-176; H. MINNS, *Catherine McAuley and the Education of Irish Roman Catholic Children in the Mid-Nineteenth Century*, in: M. HILTON & P. HIRSCH (eds.), *Practical Visionaries: Women, Education and Social Progress, 1790-1930*, Harlow, Longman, 2000, pp. 52-65.

173. M. GLEASON, *Disciplining the Student Body: Schooling and the Construction of Canadian Children's Bodies, 1930–1960*, in: *History of Education Quarterly*, 41:2 (2001), p. 198.

174. STANLEY, *Women and Education* (see note 86), made a similar observation.

175. T. O'DONOGHUE, *Child-abuse Scandals and the Catholic Church: Are We Asking the Right Historical Questions?*, in: *History of Education Review*, 32:1 (2003), p. 8. Similar ideas were

also expressed in T.A. O'DONOGHUE, *Upholding the Faith: The Process of Education in Catholic Schools in Australia 1922-1965*, New York, Peter Lang, 2001.

176. C. RHÉAUME, *La création musicale chez les religieuses enseignantes de Montréal*, in: *Les Cahiers de l'ARMuQ [Association pour l'avancement de la recherche en musique du Québec]*, 10 (June 1988), pp. 34-40.

177. LEI, "*The Science Ball*" (see note 42), pp. 9-28.

178. E. SMYTH, *Canonizing the Text: Readers, Teaching Manuals and Ontario Women Religious 1867-1920*, in: A. VAN GORP & M. DEPAEPE (eds.), *Auf der Suche nach der wahren Art von Textbüchern* (Beiträge zur historischen und systematischen Schulbuchforschung 7), Bad Heilbrunn, Verlag Julius Klinkhardt, 2008, pp. 119-127. For instances of textbooks used by teaching orders see for example J. ROUX, *L'enseignement primaire dans l'Ardèche sous la Monarchie de Juillet. La contribution des congrégations religieuses à l'enseignement élémentaire*, in: *Revue du Vivarais*, 94 (1993), pp. 125-142.

179. D. LAPERLE, "*Une parole de Dieu fraîchement exprimée*": *fondements, usages et représentations du musée scolaire dans les pensionnats de filles des Soeurs des Saints Noms de Jésus et de Marie (1843-1981)*, in: *Historical Studies in Education/Revue d'histoire de l'éducation*, 19:1 (2007), pp. 53-79.

180. W. RUBERG, *Children's Correspondence as a Pedagogical Tool in the Netherlands (1770-1850)*, in: *Paedagogica Historica*, 41:3 (2005), pp. 299, 310.

181. For the biographical approach in the history of education see E. GLASER & P. SCHMID, *Biographieforschung in der Historischen Pädagogik*, in: H.-H. KRÜGER & W. MAROTZKI (eds.), *Handbuch erziehungswissenschaftliche Biographieforschung*, 2nd ed., Wiesbaden, Vs Verlag für Sozialw., 2006, pp. 363-389; A. BOLÍVAR, J. DOMINGO & M. FERNÁNDEZ, *La investigación biográfico-narrativa en educación. Enfoque y metodología*, Madrid, La Muralla, 2001. For some reflections on the place of biographical studies in the field of the history of education see J. MARTIN & J. GOODMAN, *Individual Lives and Social Histories*, in: J. MARTIN & J. GOODMAN, *Women and Education 1800-1980. Educational Reform and Personal Identities*, Basingstoke, Palgrave Macmillan, 2004, pp. 7-26. For the life history of women teachers and feminism see S. MIDDLETON, *Schooling and Radicalisation: Life Histories of New Zealand Feminist Teachers*, in: *British Journal of Sociology of Education*, 8:2 (1987), pp. 169-189 (reprinted in: L. STONE (ed.), *The Education Feminism Reader*, London, Routledge, 1994); P. MUNRO, *Subject to Fiction: Women Teachers' Life History Narratives and the Cultural Politics of Resistance*, Buckingham, Open University Press, 1998; M. CROCCO, P. MUNRO & K. WEILER, *Pedagogies of Resistance: Women Educator Activists, 1880-1960*, New York, Teachers College Press, 1999.

182. An example which surprises in a positive way is M. SELLER, *Women Educators in the United States, 1820-1993: a Bio-bibliographical Sourcebook*, Westport, Greenwood Press, 1994, which includes biographical essays on 4 sisters.

183. E.g. R. FLAXMAN, *A Woman Styled Bold: the Life of Cornelia Connelly, 1809-1879*, London, Darton Longman & Todd, 1991; É. LAMIRANDE, *Elisabeth Bruyère, Fondatrice des Sœurs de la Charité d'Ottawa*, Montreal, Éditions Bellarmin, 1992; E.M. STRUB, *Yes, Lord, Always Yes: A Life of Cornelia Connelly 1809 - 1879, Founder of the Society of the Holy Child Jesus*, Rome, Society of the Holy Child Jesus, 2003; R. MCDOUGALL, *Cornelia Connelly: Woman of Mercy and Educator*, in: *Records of the American Catholic Historical Society of Philadelphia* 107:1-2 (1996), pp. 45-65; M. LUIRARD, *Madeleine-Sophie Barat (1779-1865). Une éducatrice au coeur du monde*, Paris, Nouvelle Cité, 1999; P. KILROY, *Madeleine-Sophie Barat, 1779-1865: A Life*, New York, Paulist Press, 2000 [translation: *Madeleine Sophie Barat. Une vie (1779-1865)*, Paris, Cerf, 2004];

P. KILROY, *The Writing of Religious Women's History: Madeleine Sophie Barat (1779-1865)*, in: RAUGHTER, *Religious Women and their History* (see note 9), pp. 9-24; M-F. CARREEL, *Sophie Barat, un projet éducatif pour aujourd'hui* (Sciences de l'éducation), Paris, Don Bosco, 2003; C. CLAIR, *La vénérable mère Julie Billiart, fondatrice et première supérieure générale de l'Institut des soeurs de Notre-Dame à Namur*, Paris, Savaète, 1986; R. MURPHY, *Julie Billiart, Woman of Courage: The Story of the Foundress of the Sisters of Notre Dame*, New York, Paulist Press, 1995; E. LEONARD, *Frances Taylor, Mother Magdalen SMG. A Portrait 1832-1900*, Roehampton, Maryfield Convent, 2005 (the Poor Servants of the Mother of God); G. HUOT, *Un rêve inouï ... des milliers de jeunes. Mère Marie-Élisabeth (1840-1881), fondatrice de la Congrégation des Sœurs de Notre-Dame du Saint-Rosaire de Rimouski*, Sainte-Foy, Anne Sigier, 1991; G. LECUIR-NEMO, *Anne-Marie Javouhey, fondatrice de la congrégation des soeurs de Saint-Joseph de Cluny (1779-1851)*, Paris, Karthala, 2001; M.C. SULLIVAN, *Catherine McAuley and the Tradition of Mercy*, Dublin, Four Courts Press, 1995; MINNS, *Catherine McAuley* (see note 172), pp. 52-65; J.R. BECK, *To Do and to Endure, the Life of Catherine Donnelly, Sister of Service*, Toronto, Dundurn Press, Toronto, 1997 (after having worked 17 years as a teaching laywoman, in 1922 she founded the Sisters of Service, a teaching order); J.R. BECK, *Sisters of Service: Breaking Free of the Monastic Tradition to Serve the Abandoned Ones*, in: *Canadian Catholic Historical Association Historical Studies*, 66 (2000), pp. 9-33 (biography of C. Donnelly); M.-É. HANOTEAU, *Une grande Nivelloise. Mère Gertrude (Justine Desbille), fondatrice des Sœurs de l'Enfant-Jésus de Nivelles, 1801-1866*, Nivelles, Institut de l'Enfant-Jésus, 1985; P. GARDINER, *An Extraordinary Australian: Mary MacKillop*, Alexandria, E J Dwyer in association with David Ell Press, 1994; M.J. OATES, *Mother Mary Katharine Drexel*, in: SELLER, *Women Educators in the United States* (see note 182); Anon., *Mère Marie-Eugénie Milleret, fondatrice des Religieuses de l'Assomption. Actes du Colloque du Centenaire, Cannes, 24-25 avril 1998*, Paris, Don Bosco, 1999; J.A.M. RECKER, *Françoise Blin De Bourdon, Woman of Influence: The Story of the Cofoundress of the Sisters of Notre Dame*, New York, Paulist Press, 2001; J.A.M. RECKER, *"Très affectueusement, votre mère en Dieu". Françoise Blin – French Aristocrat, Belgian Citizen, Co-Foundress of the Sisters of Notre Dame de Namur (1756-1838)* (Belgian Francophone Library 6), New York, Peter Lang, 2001; M.R. THIAUCOURT, *Madre Teresa de Saldanha: vida e obra*, Lisboa, Irmãs Dominicanas de Santa Catarina de Sena, 1987.

184. E.g. P. KIENLE & K. LUTZ-EFINGER, *Komm Schwester, tritt ins Licht. Schwester Philomena (Gertrud Schmittdiel), Generaloberin der Schwestern der Christlichen Liebe* (Glaube und Leben 17), Berlin, Lit-verlag, 2004; T. MITRANO, *Mother Joseph Butler*, in: SELLER, *Women Educators in the United States* (see note 182).

185. E.g. C.K. KILLERBY, *Ursula Frayne: A Biography*, Fremantle, Fremantle Arts Centre Press, 1997; M.J. OATES, *Mother Mary Regis Casserly*, in: SELLER, *Women Educators in the United States* (see note 182).

186. E.g. S. BURLEY, *Carmel Bourke RSM, O.B.E. 1907-1995*, in: *Unicorn. Journal of the Australian College of Education*, online section of *Great Australian Educators*, 2001 (City of Adelaide; Principal of Saint Aloyius College; Principal of Mercedes College; Sisters of Mercy); S. BURLEY, *Sister Carmel Bourke RSM (1907-1995): A Lens through which to Study Religious and Educational Change*, in: *Women-Church*, 40 (2007), pp. 80-85; S. BURLEY, *Sister Jillian Havey, OP. The Principal at the Priory*, in: *Unicorn. Journal of the Australian College of Education*, 23:3 (1997), pp. 71-75 (St Dominic's Priory College, North Adelaide; Dominican Sisters); M. REGAN, *Sister Jillian Havey*, in: P. DUIGNAN & D. GURR (eds.), *Leading Australia's Schools*, Sydney, ACEL and DEST, 2007.

187. E.g. E.M. SMYTH, *Sister-Professors: Roman Catholic Women Religious as Academics in English Canada, 1897-1962*, in: P. STORTZ & E.L. PANAYOTIDIS (eds.), *Historical Identities:*

The Professoriate in Canada, Toronto, University of Toronto Press, 2006, pp. 207-224 (a brief discussion of the life histories of some sister-professors in English Canada on the basis of obituaries); D.M. HALLMAN, *"Woman of Exodus II": Irene Poelzer, the Women's Movement, and Teacher Education*, in: STORTZ & PANAYOTIDIS, *Historical Identities*, pp. 225-247 (about Sister M. Ruth of the Institute of the Blessed Virgin Mary, Professor of Educational Foundations at the College of Education, University of Saskatchewan from 1970 to 1993); D.M. HALLMAN & A.H. LATHROP, *Sustaining the Fire of "Scholarly Passion": Mary G. Hamilton (1883-1972) and Irene Poelzer (1926-)*, in: E.M. SMYTH & P. BOURNE (eds.), *Women Teaching, Women Learning: Historical Perspectives*, Toronto, Inanna Publications & Education, 2006, pp. 45-64.

188. M. DERKS & R. WOLF, *Wetenschap in dienstbaarheid: Ida B.M. Frye (1909), heilpedagoge* (Vrouwen van formaat, 2), Nijmegen, Vantilt, 2000; J. EIJT, *Zuster Marie van Uden (1895-1975): Pionier in het buitengewoon onderwijs*, in: J. BROUWERS et al. (eds.), *Brabantse biografieën. Levensbeschrijvingen van bekende en onbekende Noord-Brabanders*, vol. 6, 's-Hertogenbosch, Stichting Brabantse Regionale Geschiedbeoefening, 2003; A. DÉSILETS, *Gadbois, Albine, dite Marie de Bonsecours*, in: *Dictionary of Canadian Biography* (online).

189. H. AMOUREUS & J. DE VRIES, *Zuster Marie Joseph van der Eerden (1883-1968): Stimulator van het nijverheidsonderwijs*, in: J. VAN OUDHEUSDEN et al. (eds.), *Brabantse biografieën. Levensbeschrijvingen van bekende en onbekende Noordbrabanders*, vol. 1, Meppel/Amsterdam, Uitgeverij Boom en Stichting Brabantse Regionale Geschiedbeoefening, 1992.

190. N. ROGIER, *Zuster Maria Luykx (1904-1996): Oprichtster van Talenpracticum Regina Coeli*, in: P. TIMMERMANS et al. (eds.), *Brabantse biografieën. Levensbeschrijvingen van bekende en onbekende Noord-Brabanders*, vol. 5, 's-Hertogenbosch, Stichting Brabantse Regionale Geschiedbeoefening, 1999.

191. MCDOUGALL, *Cornelia Connelly's Innovations in Female Education* (see note 123).

192. For the latter, see e.g. C. AINSLEY, *Eulalie Durocher: De l'histoire à l'imaginaire*, Laval, Éditions du Méridien, 1993; C. MAILLOUX, *Une femme dans la tourmente*, Lachine, Éditions Sainte-Anne, 1992 (about Esther Blondin).

193. *Cf.* D. MOULINET, *Les publications françaises relatives à l'histoire des congrégations religieuses*, in: DE MAEYER, LEPLAE & SCHMIEDL, *Religious Institutes in Western Europe* (see note 6), p. 56.

194. GLASER & SCHMID, *Biographieforschung* (see note 181), p. 380; G. KLUCHERT, *Biographie und Institution. Eine deutsches Gymnasium und seine Lehrer in verschiedenen politischen Systemen*, in: *Jahrbuch für Historische Bildungsforschung*, 12 (2006), p. 9.

195. E.g. M. HOLMES & B.J. WEISS, *Lives of Women Public Schoolteachers. Scenes from American Educational History*, New York, Garland Publishing, 1995 (biographical sketches of 12 women whose teaching careers spanned a century – from the 1830s to the 1960s); J.B. MARGADANT, *Madame le Professeur: Women Educators in the Third Republic*, Princeton, Princeton University Press, 1990 (first generation of female secondary schoolteachers); COPELMAN, *London's Women Teachers* (see note 23).

196. J. COLLINS, *Hidden Lives: The Teaching and Religious Lives of Eight Dominican Sisters, 1931-1961*, unpublished Master of Education thesis, Massey University, New Zealand, 2001.

197. J. COLLINS, *Strategies for Survival and Success: Dominican Teachers 1931-1961*, in: *History of Education Review*, 33:1 (2004), pp. 1-13.

198. COLLINS, *Strategies for Survival and Success* (see note 197), p. 4.

199. J. COLLINS, *Revisiting the Foucauldian Account of Power: Constraints and Opportunities in the Leadership Experience of Dominican Teachers*, in: *Delta Journal*, 57:1-2 (2005), pp. 89-102.

200. S. BURLEY, *Lost Leaders from the Convent and the Classroom 1880-1925*, in: J. MCMAHON, H. NEIDHART & J. CHAPMAN (eds.), *Leading the Catholic School*, Victoria, Spectrum 1997, pp. 49-61; BURLEY, *Past Principals* (see note 165), pp. 339-352.

201. J. GRESKO, *The 'Serfs of the System'? Oblate Brothers and the Sisters of St. Ann in British Columbia Schools, 1858-1920*, in: *Western Oblate Studies/Études oblates de l'Ouest*, 4 (1996) [= R. HUEL (ed.), *Proceedings of the Fourth Symposium on the History of the Oblates in Western and Northern Canada/Actes du quatrième colloque sur l'histoire des Oblats dans l'Ouest et le Nord canadiens, 25-26 août/August 1995*], pp. 119-141.

202. K. CASEY, *I Answer with my Life: Life Histories of Women Teachers Working for Social Change*, New York, Routledge, 1993.

203. This criticism was voiced by G. GRACE, *Women Teachers as Organic Intellectuals*, in: *British Journal of Sociology of Education*, 16:3 (1995), pp. 415-417.

204. T. HAMEL, *Teacher Training in Turmoil: The Experience of Professors in Normal Schools and Faculties of Education during the Quiet Revolution in Quebec*, in: STORTZ & PANAYOTIDIS, *Historical Identities* (see note 187), pp. 183-204.

205. This method was also used by J. PENEFF, *Autobiographies d'enseignants d'écoles publiques et privées*, in: *Les Cahiers du L.E.R.S.C.O.* 8 (January 1987). Two of the 11 autobiographical accounts are of teaching sisters.

206. E.g. M.C. SULLIVAN (ed.), *The Correspondence of Catherine McAuley, 1818-1841*, Dublin, Four Courts Press, 2004; J. HÉBERT & M.-C. DE SÉGONZAC (eds.), *Javouhey Anne-Marie: Correspondance, 1798-1851*, 4 vols., Paris, Cerf, 1994.

207. E.g. V. COHEN IMARCH, *Epistolas en busca de un lugar. Las maestras del Colegio de Educandas de Salta ante el proceso secularizador (segunda mitad del siglo xix)*, in: *Andes online* 2003.

208. MACCURTAIN, *Late in the Field* (see note 6), p. 58. WYNANTS, *Les religieuses de vie active en Belgique et aux Pays-Bas* (see note 6), pp. 255-256, also pointed out that one should urgently collect much more oral evidence from elderly women religious.

209. E.g. P. LEJEUNE, *Les instituteurs du XIXe siècle racontent leur vie*, in: *Histoire de l'éducation*, 25 (1985), pp. 53-82; P. LEJEUNE, *Répertoire des autobiographies écrites en France au XIXe siècle: vies d'instituteurs*, in: *Histoire de l'éducation*, 25 (1985), pp. 83-104 (including some autobiographies written by women teachers after 1914).

210. S. GEMIE, *Women and Schooling in France, 1815-1914. Gender, Authority and Identity in the Female Schooling Sector*, Keele, Keele University Press, 1995.

211. For theoretical considerations of what people remember of their school life see E. SOUTHGATE, *Remembering School. Mapping Continuities in Power, Subjectivity & Emotion in Stories of School Life*, New York, Peter Lang, 2003; M. SUÁREZ PAZOS, *La reconstrucció de la memòria escolar a través de les autobiografies*, in: *Educació i història: Revista d'història de l'educació*, 9-10 (2006-2007), pp. 40-48; M.M. UITTO, *Expectations and Contradictions: Teacher-Student Relationships Told in Teacher Memories*, Paper presented at *The European Conference on Educational Research (ECER): From Teaching to Learning?*, Göteborg, 10 September, 2008. For an unpublished study of the 'lived experience' of students in and around their Catholic convent classrooms see BURLEY, *Voices, Cultures and Pedagogies in Catholic Convent Classrooms: South Australia, 1880-2000* (see note 161).

212. M. HILHORST, *Bij de zusters op kostschool. Geschiedenis van het dagelijks leven van meisjes op Rooms-katholieke pensionaten in Nederland en Vlaanderen*, Utrecht, Bruna, 1989. See also: M. HILHORST, *Pas à deux mes enfants! Meisjesvriendschappen en opvoeding op kloosterpensionaten, 1920-1965*, in: *Comenius. Wetenschappelijk tijdschrift voor de democratisering van*

opvoeding, onderwijs, vorming en hulpverlening, 8:4 (1988), pp. 442-460; M. HILHORST, *Van jonge juffrouwen en kwekelingen. Katholieke meisjeskostscholen in de eerste helft van de twintigste eeuw*, in: M. GREVER & A. VAN DER VEEN (eds.), *Bij ons moeder en ons Jet. Brabantse vrouwen in de 19de en 20ste eeuw*, Zutphen, Walburgpers, 1989, pp. 100-121; J. EIJT & M. HILHORST, *"Een geïsoleerde opvoeding". Zusters en leerlingen op katholieke meisjespensionaten*, in: *"En Marie werd wijzer..." Culturele verschijningsvormen van meisjesonderwijs in heden en verleden*, Nijmegen, Vereniging Landelijk Overleg Vrouwengeschiedenis, 1989, pp. 71-84; M. HILHORST, *Op kostschool bij de nonnen 1920-1965*, in: M. GREVER et al. (eds.), *Vrouwendomein. Woongeschiedenis van vrouwen in Nederland* (Tipje van de sluier 4), Amsterdam, Uitgeverij Sua, 1986, pp. 108-122.

213. DUMONT & FAHMY-EID, *Les couventines* (see note 48).

214. M. DUMONT, *Grandir au pensionnat au Québec au tournant des années 1950*, in: *Historical Studies in Education/Revue d'histoire de l'éducation*, 20:2 (2008), pp. 111-121.

215. BENNETT & FORGAN, *Convent Girls* (see note 85).

216. *Cf.* the contrasting experiences of two American women who attended schools run by the Society of the Sacred Heart. One described life at the school as "closely aligned to that in a penal colony" (V.V. HARRISON, *Changing Habits: A Memoir of the Society of the Sacred Heart*, New York, Doubleday, 1988), whereas the other spoke with enthusiasm about her school days (SIGMUND, *Sanctuary or prison?* (see note 164)).

217. L. BIENVENUE & C. HUDON, *"Pour devenir homme, tu transgresseras... ". Quelques enjeux de la socialisation masculine dans les collèges classiques québécois (1880-1939)*, in: *Canadian Historical Review*, 86:3 (2005), pp. 485-511 (based on 60 memoirs and autobiographies written by former pupils).

218. For a memoir which includes the author's time as a student at the Forest Ridge School of the Sacred Heart see M. MCCARTHY, *Memories of a Catholic Girlhood*, San Diego, Harcourt Brace, 1974. Another category of sources is fictional accounts written by alumnae of schools administered by sisters, for example A. WHITE, *Frost in May*, New York, Dial Press, 1933, a novel set in a British Sacred Heart school, loosely modelled on the school the author attended. Both instances are taken from I. DEBARE, *Where Girls Come First: The Rise, Fall, and Surprising Revival of Girls' Schools*, New York, Jeremy P. Tarcher/Penguin, 2004. For a biographical account of the graduate of St. Joseph's Academy who founded the school's Alumnae Association and its literary magazine see E. SMYTH, *Gertrude Lawler and St Joseph's Academy: Alumnae, Advocate and Author*, in: *Canadian Catholic Historical Association Historical Studies*, 72 (2006), pp. 124-141.

219. GREW & HARRIGAN, *The Catholic Contribution to Universal Schooling in France, 1850-1906* (see note 57), p. 233.

220. P. SAVOIE, A. BRUTER & W. FRIJHOFF, *Secondary Education: Institutional, Cultural and Social History*, in: *Paedagogica Historica*, 40:1-2 (2004), p. 11.

221. P. WYNANTS, *La collaboration entre laïcs et religieuses enseignantes en Belgique. Esquisse historique (XIXe-XXe siècles)*, in: *Vie consacrée*, 60:3 (1988), p. 162.

222. CURTIS, *Educating the Faithful* (see note 58).

223. A.T. QUARTARARO, *Women Teachers and Popular Education in Nineteenth-Century France. Social Values and Corporate Identity at the Normal School Institution*, Newark, University of Delaware Press, 1995.

224. C. DE BELLAIGUE, *Behind the School Walls: The School Community in French and English Boarding Schools for Girls, 1810-1867*, in: *Paedagogica Historica*, 40:1-2 (2004), pp. 107-121; C. DE BELLAIGUE, *Educating Women. Schooling and Identity in England and France, 1800-1867*, Oxford, Oxford University Press, 2007.

225. E. SMYTH, *"Much Exertion of the Voice and Great Application of the Mind". Teacher Education within the Congregation of the Sisters of St. Joseph of Toronto, Canada, 1851-1920*, in: *Historical Studies in Education/Revue d'histoire de l'éducation*, 6:3 (1994), pp. 97-113; E. SMYTH, *"Developing the Powers of the Youthful Mind"* (see note 147), pp. 111-116, 123; E. SMYTH, *Professionalization among the Professed: The Case of Roman Catholic Women Religious*, in: E.M. SMYTH, A. PRENTICE, S. ACKER & P. BOURNE (eds.), *Challenging Professions: Women and the Professions in English Canada*, Toronto, University of Toronto Press, 1999, pp. 234-254; ROGERS, *From the Salon to the Schoolroom* (see note 59); R. ROGERS, *Les enseignantes religieuses et laïques au XIXe siècle: vocation ou activité professionnelle*, in: J.-Y. CAUSER, R. PFEFFERKORN & B. WOEHL, *Métiers, identités professionnelles et genre*, Paris, L'Harmattan, 2007, pp. 33-50; ROGERS, *Questioning National Models* (see note 44); GALUSH, *What Should Janek Learn?* (see note 158), pp. 395-417; MATTINGLY, *Uncovering Forgotten Habits* (see note 154), pp. 160-181. See also COBURN & SMITH, *Spirited Lives* (see note 87); CURTIS, *Educating the Faithful* (see note 58).

226. MANGION, *"Good Teacher" or "Good Religious"?* (see note 14), pp. 223-239.

227. F. MAYEUR, *La formation des institutrices avant la loi Paul Bert. Les cours normaux*, in: CHOLVY & CHALINE, *L'enseignement catholique en France* (see note 73), p. 121; CURTIS, *Educating the Faithful* (see note 58).

228. This point was raised by MATTINGLY, *Uncovering Forgotten Habits* (see note 154), pp. 160-181.

229. MANGION, *"Good Teacher" or "Good Religious"?* (see note 14), p. 227.

230. VAN DRENTH & VAN ESSEN, *The Ambiguity of Professing Gender* (see note 11), p. 394.

231. For the increasing adoption of state models of teacher training in New Zealand see J. COLLINS, *From 'Apprentice' to 'Professional': The Training of New Zealand Catholic Teachers 1945-65*, in: *History of Education Review*, 34:2 (2005), pp. 27-40.

232. ROGERS, *Questioning National Models* (see note 44). For the Netherlands see note 73.

233. ROGERS, *Retrograde or Modern?* (see note 14), 157, 161.

234. DANYLEWYCZ, *Taking the Veil* (see note 87), p. 96.

235. WHITE, *Maintaining Anglo-Celtic Cultural Hegemony in Saskatchewan* (see note 160), pp. 253-279.

236. V.A. MCCLELLAND, *Review of C. Dyhouse, Girls Growing Up in Late Victorian and Edwardian England (London/Boston: Routledge/Kegan Paul, 1981) and A. Digby & P. Searby, Children, School and Society in Nineteenth Century Engeland (London/Basingstoke: Macmillan, 1981)*, in: *Victorian Studies*, 27:1 (1983), pp. 107-108.

237. O'HAGAN, *The Contribution of the Religious Orders* (see note 50), p. 156.

238. LUC, *L'invention du jeune enfant* (see note 55), pp. 312, 336.

239. DÉSILETS, *Gadbois* (see note 188).

240. For a 20th century example see VAN DRENTH & VAN ESSEN, *The Ambiguity of Professing Gender* (see note 11).

241. WALL, *"Definite Lines of Influence"* (see note 74).

242. E. LAMONTAGNE & Y. COHEN, *Les Soeurs Grises à l'Université de Montréal, 1923-1947: de la gestion hospitalière à l'enseignement supérieur en nursing*, in: *Historical Studies in Education/Revue d'histoire de l'éducation*, 15:2 (2003), pp. 273-297. See also Y. COHEN, *La Contribution des Soeurs de la Charité à la Modernisation de l'Hôpital Notre-Dame, 1880–1940*, in: *Canadian Historical Review*, 77:2 (1996), pp. 185-220.

243. OATES, *"The Good Sisters"* (see note 50), p. 184; SMYTH, *"Much Exertion of the Voice and Great Application of the Mind"* (see note 225), p. 112.

244. R. ROGERS, *Boarding Schools, Women Teachers, and Domesticity: Reforming Girls' Secondary Education in the First Half of the Nineteenth Century*, in: *French Historical Studies*, 19:1 (1995), p. 175.

245. DANYLEWYCZ, *Taking the Veil* (see note 87), pp. 97-103; BURLEY, *Lost Leaders from the Convent and the Classroom* (see note 200), pp. 51-52; ROGERS, *Retrograde or Modern?* (see note 14), p. 159.

246. See e.g. L.M. GOOLEY MCPHERON, *A Historical Perspective of Career Patterns of Women in the Teaching Profession: 1900-1940*, PhD dissertation, Illinois State University, 1981; M.F. WHITELY, *Annie Leake's Occupation: Development of a Teaching Career, 1858-1886*, in: *Historical Studies in Education/Revue d'histoire de l'éducation*, 4:1 (1992), pp. 97-112.

247. ROGERS, *Retrograde or Modern?* (see note 14), pp. 159-160.

248. DANYLEWYCZ, *Taking the Veil* (see note 87), pp. 97-103.

249. MALOUIN, *Ma soeur, à quelle école allez-vous?* (see note 84), pp. 45-49, 152.

250. C. LANGLOIS, *Le catholicisme au féminin. Les congrégations françaises à supérieure générale au XIXe siècle*, Paris, Cerf, 1984.

251. OATES, *"The Good Sisters"* (see note 50), pp. 180-181.

252. BURLEY, *Lost Leaders from the Convent and the Classroom* (see note 245), p. 52; BURLEY, *Past Principals* (see note 165), pp. 348-349.

253. ROGERS, *From the Salon to the Schoolroom* (see note 59), p. 136.

254. M. THIVIERGE, *La syndicalisation des institutrices catholiques, 1900-1959*, in: FAHMY-EID & DUMONT, *Maîtresses de maison* (see note 56), pp. 171-189.

255. L. VAN ROMPAEY, *Strijd voor waardering*, Antwerpen, Garant, 2003, pp. 232-238. See also L. MINTEN, *"De besten onder de goeden": 175 jaar zusters der Christelijke Scholen Vorselaar*, in: *Basis: Ledenblad van het COV*, 103:11 (8 juni 1996), pp. 40-41.

256. BURLEY, *Past Principals* (see note 165), p. 345; STANLEY, *Women and Education at St. Ann's Academy* (see note 86).

257. P. AUBIN, *Les communautés religieuses et l'édition du manuel scolaire au Quebec, 1765-1964* (Cahiers du GRÉLQ 8), Sherbrooke, Ex Libris, 2001.

258. See e.g. A. LABARRÈRE-PAULÉ, *L'instituteur laïque canadien français au 19ème siècle*, in: *Report of the Annual Meeting/Rapports annuels de la Société historique du Canada*, 42:1 (1963), pp. 102-115; A. LABARRÈRE-PAULÉ, *Les instituteurs laïques au Canada français, 1836-1900*, Quebec, Presses de l'Université Laval, 1965.

259. T. HAMEL, *La production pédagogique des Sœurs de la Congrégation de Notre-Dame: 1858-1991*, in: *SCHEC Études d'histoire religieuse*, 65 (1999), pp. 67-87.

260. GALUSH, *What Should Janek Learn?* (see note 158), p. 413.

261. LANGLOIS, *Le catholicisme au féminin* (see note 250).

262. LANGLOIS, *La fabrique des enseignantes* (see note 49), pp. 163-169.

263. A notable exception is our own studies about the feminization of the teaching profession in Belgium: see note 1.

264. M.-P. MALOUIN, *La laïcisation de l'école publique québécoise entre 1939 et 1969: un processus de masculinisation*, in: *Historical Studies in Education/Revue d'histoire de l'éducation*, 4:1 (1992), pp. 1-29. *Cf.* C. BAUDOUX, *La gestion en éducation, une affaire d'hommes ou de femmes?*, Cap-Rouge, Les Presses Inter Universitaires, 1994.

265. D. STAPLETON, *A Changing of the Guard: The Change of Leadership of Catholic Secondary Schools in Post World War II Victoria*, Paper presented at the *AARE [The Australian Association for Research in Education] Conference*, Adelaide, 1998.

266. PRENTICE & THEOBALD, *The Historiography of Women Teachers: A Retrospect* (see note 25), p. 23.

267. BURLEY, *Past Principals* (see note 165).

268. M. DANYLEWYCZ, B. LIGHT & A. PRENTICE, *The Evolution of the Sexual Division of Labour in Teaching: A Nineteenth-century Ontario and Quebec Case Study*, in: *Histoire sociale/Social History*, 16 (1983), pp. 94, 108.

269. MARGADANT, *Madame le Professeur* (see note 195), pp. 10, 24.

270. DE BELLAIGUE, *Behind the School Walls* (see note 224), pp. 114, 118, 121.

271. SMYTH, *"Much Exertion of the Voice and Great Application of the Mind"* (see note 225), p. 112.

272. For the latter see the remarks by O'DONOGHUE, *Come Follow Me and Forsake Temptation* (see note 53).

273. M.-P. MALOUIN, *Que sont devenues les sœurs de nos écoles? Recherche sur les orientations actuelles des religieuses enseignantes au Québec*, Sherbrooke, Association des religieuses enseignantes du Québec (AREQ), 1989.

274. *Cf.* for example the remarks about J. Eijt's studies by WYNANTS, *België en Nederland op gescheiden wegen?* (see note 6), pp. 68-69. For feminist studies of women religious see Y. TURIN, *Femmes et religieuses au XIXème siècle: le féminisme 'en religion'*, Paris, Nouvelle Cité, 1989; DUMONT, *Une perspective féministe* (see note 6); DUMONT, *Les religieuses sont-elles féministes?* (see note 48).

275. E.g. M. SCHWEGMAN, *De strijd tegen de "mannelijke" blik. Vrouwengeschiedenis als eindexamenonderwerp*, in: *Tijdschrift voor Vrouwenstudies*, 11:2 (1990), p. 189.

Bibliography

ACKERMANS, G., *Vereeniging van vrouwen...Franciscanessen van Heythuysen in Nederland (1900-1975)*, Heythuysen, Provincialaat Franciscanessen van Heythuysen, 1994.

AINSLEY, C., *Eulalie Durocher: De l'histoire à l'imaginaire*, Laval, Éditions du Méridien, 1993.

ALBINO BENCOSTTA, M.L. (ed.), *História da Educação, Arquitetura e Espaço Escolar*, São Paulo, Cortez Editora, 2005.

ALEJO MONTES, J., *Review of I. Azcárate Rístori, El Monasterio de la Enseñanza de Barcelona, 1645-1876 (Barcelona, 1993)*, in: *Historia de la Educación*, 12-13 (1993-1994), pp. 618-619.

ALLISON, D.R. & PLOUFFE, H., *Convent Schools*, in: *Encyclopedia of Music in Canada*, www.thecanadianencyclopedia.com/index.cfm?PgNm=TCE&Params=U1SEC837247.

AMOUREUS, H. & DE VRIES, J., *Zuster Marie Joseph van der Eerden (1883-1968): Stimulator van het nijverheidsonderwijs*, in: J. VAN OUDHEUSDEN et al. (eds.), *Brabantse biografieën. Levensbeschrijvingen van bekende en onbekende Noordbrabanders*, vol. 1, Meppel/Amsterdam, Uitgeverij Boom en Stichting Brabantse Regionale Geschiedbeoefening, 1992.

ANDREW, S., *Selling Education: The Problems of Convent Schools in Acadian New Brunswick, 1858-1886*, in: *Canadian Catholic Historical Association Historical Studies*, 62 (1996), pp. 15-32.

— *Gender and Nationalism: Acadians, Québécois, and Irish in New Brunswick Nineteenth-Century Colleges and Convent Schools, 1854-1888*, in: *Canadian Catholic Historical Association Historical Studies*, 68 (2002), pp. 7-23.

ANNAERT, P., *Les collèges au féminin. Les Ursulines: enseignement et vie consacrée aux XVIIe et XVIIIe siècles*, Namur, Vie consacrée, 1992.

Anon., *Book note of G. Ramis (ed.), I Simposium d'Historia social del segle XIX. Aproximació a Sor María Rafela del Sgt. Cor i al seu entorn religiós i històric (1814-1899), Caixa de Balears, 1999*, in: *Boletín de Historia de la Educación*, 32 (2000).

Anon., *Festschrift des St.-Franziskus-Gymnasiums in Olpe. Aus Anlaß der Wiedereröffnung vor 100 Jahren*, Olpe, St.-Franziskus-Gymnasium, 1993.

Anon., *Les congrégations religieuses et la société française d'un siècle à l'autre. Actes du colloque des 17-18 octobre 2003*, Paris, Don Bosco, 2004.

Anon., *Mère Marie-Eugénie Milleret, fondatrice des Religieuses de l'Assomption. Actes du Colloque du Centenaire, Cannes, 24-25 avril 1998*, Paris, Don Bosco, 1999.

AUBIN, P., *Les communautés religieuses et l'édition du manuel scolaire au Quebec, 1765-1964* (Cahiers du GRÉLQ 8), Sherbrooke, Ex Libris, 2001.

AUMANN, F. et al., *150 jaar Zusters van Liefde te Sint-Truiden*, Sint-Truiden, Psychiatrisch Ziekenhuis Sancta Maria v.z.w. Sint-Truiden, 1991.

BARBARO, A., *Recovering the Origins of Convent Education in Australia*, in: *Journal of the Australian Catholic Historical Society*, 24 (2003), pp. 45-56.

BAUDOUX, C., *La gestion en éducation, une affaire d'hommes ou de femmes?*, Cap-Rouge, Les Presses Inter Universitaires, 1994.

BAUMGARTEN, N., *Immigrants as Democrats: Education in St. Louis before the Civil War*, unpublished PhD dissertation, Harvard University, 1993.

— *Education and Democracy in Frontier St. Louis: The Society of the Sacred Heart*, in: *History of Education Quarterly*, 34 (1994), pp. 171-192.

— *Catholic Teaching Orders*, in: L. EISENMANN (ed.), *Historical Dictionary of Women's Education in the United States*, Westport, Greenwood Press, 1998, pp. 71-74.

BEADIE, N., *Toward a History of Education Markets in the United States. An Introduction*, in: *Social Science History*, 32:1 (2008), pp. 47-73.

BECK, J.R., *To Do and to Endure, the Life of Catherine Donnelly, Sister of Service*, Toronto, Dundurn Press, Toronto, 1997.

— *Sisters of Service: Breaking Free of the Monastic Tradition to Serve the Abandoned Ones*, in: *Canadian Catholic Historical Association Historical Studies*, 66 (2000), pp. 9-33.

BENNETT, J. & FORGAN, R. (eds.), *Convent Girls*, London, Virago, 2003 (updated and revised edition of *There's Something about a Convent Girl*, London, Virago, 1991).

BIANCHI, A. & ROCCA, G. (eds.), *L'educazione femminile tra cinque e settecento*, in: *Annali di Storia dell'Educazione e delle Istituzioni Scolastiche*, 14 (2007), pp. 11-176.

BIENVENUE, L. & HUDON, C., *"Pour devenir homme, tu transgresseras... ". Quelques enjeux de la socialisation masculine dans les collèges classiques québécois (1880-1939)*, in: *Canadian Historical Review*, 86:3 (2005), pp. 485-511.

BOLÍVAR, A., DOMINGO, J. & FERNÁNDEZ, M., *La investigación biográfico-narrativa en educación. Enfoque y metodología*, Madrid, La Muralla, 2001.

BOMBARDIER, J. & LAPAGE, A.-M. (eds.), *Histoire des soeurs de la Doctrine Chrétienne de Nancy*, 5 vols., Nancy, Doctrine Chrétienne, 1995.

BOUILLÉ, L., *Séparation de l'Église et de l'État. Les Ursulines de Château-Gontier*, in: *L'Oribus*, 56 (2002), pp. 3-20.

BOURGEOIS, I., *The Rideau Street Convent School: French-language Private Schooling in Ontario*, in: S.A. COOK, L.R. MCLEAN & K. O'ROURKE (eds.), *Framing Our Past: Canadian Women's History in the Twentieth Century*, Montreal and Kingston, McGill-Queen's University Press, 2001, pp. 178-183, 455-456.

BOWDEN, C., *"For the Glory of God": a Study of the Education of English Catholic Women in Convents in Flanders and France in the First Half of the Seventeenth Century*, in: J. COOLAHAN, R. ALDRICH & F. SIMON (eds.), *Faiths and Education: Historical and Comparative Perspectives* (*Paedagogica Historica* Supplementary Series 5), Gent, CSHP, 1999, pp. 77-95.

— *Community Space and Cultural Transmission: Formation and Schooling in English Enclosed Convents in the Seventeenth Century*, in: *History of Education*, 34:4 (2005), pp. 365-386.

BOWMAN, L.M.A., *Women in Religious Education: The Cause of Cornelia Connelly*, in: *The Living Light*, 27:3 (1991), pp. 240-247.

— *Women's Religious Education: Liberation or Socialization? A Case Study*, in: *Religious Education*, 88:1 (1993), pp. 22-38.

— *The History of Women, Religion and Education: A Methodological Approach*, in: *Toronto Journal of Theology*, 11:2 (1995), pp. 201-216.

BRASIL SILVA, M. & INÁCIO FILHO, G., *O Curso Normal Do Colégio Sagrado Coração De Jesus – 1931-1947, processo pedagógico*, in: *Revista HISTEDBR On-line*, 15 (September 2004).

BRAUN, P., *Lehrschwestern und Schulbrüder im Ablauf des Kulturkampfes in der Schweiz (1866-1884)*, in: *Rottenburger Jahrbuch für Kirchengeschichte*, 15 (1996), pp. 115-126.

BRAUN, P. (ed.), *Die Kongregationen in der Schweiz 19. und 20. Jahrhundert* (Helvetica Sacra 8.2), Basel, Schwabe, 1998.

BREWER, E.M., *Nuns and the Education of American Catholic Women, 1860-1920*, Chicago, Loyola University Press, 1987.

BREY ALVAREZ, M.L., *Una educadora novohispana: María Ignacia de Azlor y Echeverz*, Bogotá, CELAM, 1989.

BROEKHUIZEN, J. (ed.), *Van mystiek naar methode: de "nonnen van Vught"*, Vught, Taleninstituut Regina Coeli, 2003.

BROSNAN, K.A., *Public Presence, Public Silence: Nuns, Bishops, and the Gendered Space of Early Chicago*, in: *Catholic Historical Review*, 90:3 (2004), pp. 473-496.

BRUNO-JOFRÉ, R., *The Oblate Sisters, A Manitoba Order: Reconstructing Early Years, 1904-1915*, in: R. BRUNO-JOFRÉ (ed.), *Issues in the History of Education in Manitoba*, Lewiston, The Edwin Mellen Press, 1993, pp. 511-567.

— *Lifting the Veil: The Founding of the Missionary Oblate Sisters of the Sacred Heart and Mary Immaculate in Manitoba*, in: *Historical Studies in Education/Revue d'histoire de l'éducation*, 9:1 (1997), pp. 1-20.

— *The Missionary Oblate Sisters: Vision and Mission*, Montreal/Kingston, McGill-Queen's Press, 2005.

BURKE, C. (ed.), *Containing the School Child: Architectures and Pedagogies*, Special issue of *Paedagogica Historica*, 41:4-5 (2005).

BURLBAW, L.M. & FIELD, S.L. (eds.), *Explorations in Curriculum History Research*, Greenwich, CT: Information Age Publishing, 2005.

BURLEY, S., *Sister Jillian Havey, OP. The Principal at the Priory*, in: *Unicorn. Journal of the Australian College of Education*, 23:3 (1997), pp. 71-75.

— *Lost Leaders from the Convent and the Classroom 1880-1925*, in: J. MCMAHON, H. NEIDHART & J. CHAPMAN (eds.), *Leading the Catholic School*, Victoria, Spectrum 1997, pp. 49-61.

— *Past Principals: "The Public Pervasive Presence of Powerful Women in the Church" in South Australia, 1880-1925*, in: J. COOLAHAN, R. ALDRICH & F. SIMON (eds.), *Faiths and Education: Historical and Comparative Perspectives* (*Paedagogica Historica* Supplementary Series 5), Gent, CSHP, 1999, pp. 339-352.

— *Carmel Bourke RSM, O.B.E. 1907-1995*, in: *Unicorn. Journal of the Australian College of Education*, online section of *Great Australian Educators*, 2001.

— *Resurrecting the Religious Experiences of Catholic Girls' Schooling in South Australia in the 1920s*, in: *Education Research and Perspectives*, 28:1 (2001), pp. 25-44.

— *Voices, Cultures and Pedagogies in Catholic Convent Classrooms: South Australia, 1880-2000*, unpublished paper presented at *ISCHE 26: New Education: Genesis and Metamorphoses*, Geneva, 2004.

— *An Overview of the Historiography of Women Religious in Australia*, in: *Journal of the Australian Catholic Historical Society*, 26 (2005), pp. 43-60.

— *Sister Carmel Bourke RSM (1907-1995): A Lens through which to Study Religious and Educational Change*, in: *Women-Church*, 40 (2007), pp. 80-85.

— *Silences and Images in an Australian Catholic School History*, in: *History of Education Researcher*, 79 (2007), pp. 2-10.

BURLEY, S. & TEAGUE, K., *Chapel, Cloister & Classroom: Reflections on the Dominican Sisters at North Adelaide*, Adelaide, Lutheran Publishing House, 1993.

BYRNE, P., *A Tradition of Educating Women: The Religious of the Sacred Heart and Higher Education*, in: *U.S. Catholic Historian*, 13:4 (1995), pp. 49-79.

CABANEL, P. & DURAND, J.-D. (eds.), *Le grand exil des congrégations religieuses françaises 1901-1914*, Paris, Cerf, 2005.

CADA, L. et al., *Shaping the Coming Age of Religious Life*, New York, Seabury, 1979.

CADOTTE, R. & COLETTE, N., *L'école Notre-Dame-de-l'Assomption, Louis-Jolliet,* Montreal, Commission scolaire de Montréal, 2001.

CAMERON, J.D., *For the People: A History of St. Francis Xavier University*, Montreal/Kingston, McGill-Queen's Press, 1996.

CAMPBELL, T.W., *The Sisters of the Church and the Anglican Diocese of Sydney, 1892-1893: A Controversy*, in: *The Journal of Religious History*, 25:2 (2001), pp. 188-206.

CANTWELL, M., *North to Share*, Victoria, The Sisters of Saint Ann, 1992.

CARREEL, M-F., *Sophie Barat, un projet éducatif pour aujourd'hui* (Sciences de l'éducation), Paris, Don Bosco, 2003.

CASEY, K., *I Answer with my Life: Life Histories of Women Teachers Working for Social Change*, New York, Routledge, 1993.

CASEY, S.E., *Held in our Hearts: A Story of the Sisters of Mercy of the Goulburn Congregation*, Braddon, Sisters of Mercy Goulburn Congregation, 2000.

CASTAGNET, V., *La formation religieuse reçue par les soeurs des congrégations enseignantes: une évidence pour les ursulines de Belgique, France et Nouvelle-France aux XVIIe et XVIIIe siècles?*, unpublished paper presented at the *Journée d'études 'Religion, fait religieux et laïcité dans la formation des enseignants (XVIe-XXe siècles)'*, Lille, 14 November, 2008.

CHAMPAGNE, L. & DUMONT, M., *Le financement d'un séminaire diocésain: le Séminaire de Sherbrooke, 1915-1950. Comparaison avec le financement des pensionnats de religieuses*, in: *Historical Studies in Education/Revue d'histoire de l'éducation*, 2:2 (1990), pp. 339-351.

CHRISTENS, R., *100 jaar Heilig-Hartinstituut Annuntiaten Heverlee. Geschiedenis van een school en een congregatie*, Leuven, Annuntiaten – KADOC, 1994.

— *Terra incognita. 75 jaar annuntiaten in Afrika*, Tielt, Lannoo, 2006 [translation: *Terra incognita. 75 ans de présence annonciade en Afrique*, Tielt, Lannoo, 2006].

CLAIR, C., *La vénérable mère Julie Billiart, fondatrice et première supérieure générale de l'Institut des soeurs de Notre-Dame à Namur*, Paris, Savaète, 1986.

CLARK, E., *Masterless Mistresses: The New Orleans Ursulines and the Development of a New World Society, 1727-1834*, Chapel Hill, University of North Carolina Press, 2007.

CLEAR, C., *Nuns in Nineteenth Century Ireland*, Dublin, Gill & Macmillan, 1987.

COBURN, C.K., *An Overview of the Historiography of Women Religious: A Twenty-Five-Year Retrospective*, in: *U.S. Catholic Historian*, 22:1 (2004), pp. 1-26.

COBURN, C.K. & SMITH, M., *Spirited Lives: How Nuns Shaped Catholic Culture and American Life, 1836-1920*, Chapel Hill, University of North Carolina Press, 1999.

COHEN, Y., *La Contribution des Soeurs de la Charité à la Modernisation de l'Hôpital Notre-Dame, 1880–1940*, in: *Canadian Historical Review*, 77:2 (1996), pp. 185-220.

COHEN IMARCH, V., *Epistolas en busca de un lugar. Las maestras del Colegio de Educandas de Salta ante el proceso secularizador (segunda mitad del siglo xix)*, in: *Andes online* 2003.

COLLINS, J., *Hidden Lives: The Teaching and Religious Lives of Eight Dominican Sisters, 1931-1961*, unpublished Master of Education thesis, Massey University, New Zealand, 2001.

— *Strategies for Survival and Success: Dominican Teachers 1931-1961*, in: *History of Education Review*, 33:1 (2004), pp. 1-13.

— *Revisiting the Foucauldian Account of Power: Constraints and Opportunities in the Leadership Experience of Dominican Teachers*, in: *Delta Journal*, 57:1-2 (2005), pp. 89-102.

— *Schooling for Faith, Citizenship and Social Mobility: Catholic Secondary Education in New Zealand, 1924-1944*, in: *Journal of Educational Administration and History*, 37:2 (2005), pp. 157-172.

— *From 'Apprentice' to 'Professional': The Training of New Zealand Catholic Teachers 1945-65*, in: *History of Education Review*, 34:2 (2005), pp. 27-40.

COMPÈRE, M.-M., *Review of P. ANNAERT, Les collèges au féminin. Les Ursulines: enseignement et vie consacrée aux XVIIe et XVIIIe siècles (Namur: Vie consacrée, 1992)*, in: *Histoire de l'éducation*, 57 (1993), p. 117.

— *L'histoire de l'éducation en Europe: essai comparatif sur la façon dont elle s'écrit*, Paris, INRP, 1995.

CONDON, B., *A Church in Entropy: Catholic Adelaide, 1868-1873*, in: *Historical Studies in Education/Revue d'histoire de l'éducation*, 6:3 (1994), pp. 115-137 [= *History of Education Review*, 23:3 (1994), pp. 115-137].

CONEJEROS MALDONADO, J.P., *Iglesia y educación. Las congregaciones religiosas de origen francés y su presencia en la educación. Chile: 1830-1912*, in: *Revista HISTEDBR On-line*, 26 (2007), pp. 25-38.

CONRAD, A., *Weibliche Lehrorden und katholische höhere Mädchenschulen im 17. Jahrhundert*, in: E. KLEINAU & C. OPITZ (eds.), *Geschichte der Mädchen- und Frauenbildung*, vol. 1: *Vom Mittelalter bis zur Aufklärung*, Frankfurt, Campus, 1996, pp. 252-262.

— *Die weiblichen "Devoten" als Instrumente der konfessionellen Erziehung in Frankreich und Deutschland*, in: H. SCHILLING (ed.), *Spannungsfeld von Staat und Kirche. "Minderheiten" und "Erziehung" im deutsch-französischen Gesellschaftsvergleich. 16. - 18. Jahrhundert*, Berlin, Duncker & Humblot, 2003, pp. 191-214.

COPELMAN, D., *London's Women Teachers: Gender, Class and Feminism, 1870-1930*, London, Routledge, 1996.

CORCORAN, T., *Mount Saint Vincent University: A Vision Unfolding, 1873-1988*, Lanham, University Press of America, 1999.

CORTADA ANDREU, E., *Ser mestra a la Catalunya del segle XIX. L'escola pública com a espai professional transgressor*, Lleida, Pagès editors, 2006.

COSTIN, M.G., *Priceless Spirit: A History of the Sisters of the Holy Cross, 1841-1893*, Notre Dame, University of Notre Dame Press, 1994.

COURIAUD, G., *La Présentation de Marie sous la Troisième République*, in: B. WACHÉ (ed.), *L'histoire des croyants. Mémoire vivante des hommes. Mélanges Charles Molette*, vol. 2, Abbeville, Paillart, 1989, pp. 719-732.

CROCCO, M., MUNRO, P. & WEILER, K., *Pedagogies of Resistance: Women Educator Activists, 1880-1960*, New York, Teachers College Press, 1999.

CRONE, M.-L., *Die Auflösung katholischer Ordensschulen für Mädchen im Bistum Limburg während der Nationalsozialistischen Herrschaft*, in: *Archiv für mittelrheinische Kirchengeschichte*, 42 (1990), pp. 237-252.

CURTIS, S.A., *Lay Habits: Religious Teachers and the Secularization Crisis of 1901-1904*, in: *French History*, 9:4 (1995), pp. 478-498.

— *Supply and Demand: Religious Schooling in Nineteenth-Century France*, in: *History of Education Quarterly*, 39:1 (1999), pp. 51-72.

— *Educating the Faithful: Religion, Schooling, and Society in Nineteenth Century France*, DeKalb, Northern Illinois University Press, 2000 [translation: *L'enseignement au temps des congrégations. Le diocèse de Lyon (1801-1905)*, Lyon, Presses universitaires de Lyon, 2003].

— *Persécution et résistance, les congrégations enseignantes face à la loi sur les associations de 1901*, in: *Revue d'histoire de l'Église de France*, 88:1 (2002), pp. 175-195.

DAIGLER, M.J., *Through the Windows: A History of the Work of Higher Education among the Sisters of Mercy of the Americas*, Scranton, University of Scranton Press, 2000.

D'AINVAL, C., *Le couvent des Oiseaux. Ces jeunes filles de bonne famille*, Paris, Perrin, 1991.

D'ALLAIRE, M., *Les communautés religieuses de Montréal, tome 2: Les communautés religieuses et l'éducation à Montréal, 1657-1900*, Montreal, Éditions du Méridien, 2002.

DANYLEWYCZ, M., *Taking the Veil: An Alternative to Marriage, Motherhood and Spinsterhood in Quebec, 1840-1920* (The Canadian Social History Series), Toronto, MacClelland & Stewart, 1987 [translation: *Profession: religieuse: un choix pour les Québécoises, 1840-1920*, Montreal, Boréal, 1988].

DANYLEWYCZ, M., LIGHT, B. & PRENTICE, A., *The Evolution of the Sexual Division of Labour in Teaching: A Nineteenth-century Ontario and Quebec Case Study*, in: *Histoire sociale/Social History*, 16 (1983), pp. 81-109.

DEACON, F., *More than Just a Shoe String and a Prayer: How Women Religious Helped Finance the Nineteenth-Century Social Fabric*, in: *U.S. Catholic Historian*, 14:1 (1996) [= special issue *Beyond the Walls: Women Religious in American Life*], pp. 67-89.

DE AZCÁRATE RISTORI, I., *El Monasterio de la Enseñanza de Barcelona, 1645-1876*, Barcelona, PPU, 1993.

DEBARE, I., *Where Girls Come First: The Rise, Fall, and Surprising Revival of Girls' Schools*, New York, Jeremy P. Tarcher/Penguin, 2004.

DE BELLAIGUE, C., *Behind the School Walls: The School Community in French and English Boarding Schools for Girls, 1810-1867*, in: *Paedagogica Historica*, 40:1-2 (2004), pp. 107-121.

— *Educating Women. Schooling and Identity in England and France, 1800-1867*, Oxford, Oxford University Press, 2007.

DE CHARRY, J., *La Société du Sacré-Cœur Institut contemplatif et apostolique*, in: *Les religieuses enseignantes XVI - XX siècles. Actes de la quatrième rencontre d'histoire religieuse organisée à Fontevraud le 4 octobre 1980 par le Centre de Recherche d'Histoire Religieuse et d'Histoire des Idées (Université d'Angers) et le Centre Culturel de l'Ouest, Université d'Angers* (Publications du Centre de recherches d'histoire religieuse et d'histoire des idées 4), Angers, Presses de l'Université d'Angers, 1981, pp. 127-135.

DELAMONT, S., *The Beech-covered Hillside: Self-presentation in the Histories of the Girls' Schools*, in: G. WALFORD (ed.), *The Private Schooling of Girls. Past and Present*, London, Woburn Press, 1993, pp. 79-100.

DE LIMA MANÇUR LINS, L., *Um olhar sobre o Colégio Santíssimo Sacramento (1940 – 1960) – Alguns aspectos da educação feminina em Alagoinhas-BA*, in: *Revista HISTEDBR On-line*, 21 (March 2006).

DELORME, M.-J., *Les rapports entre le pensionnat Sainte-Marie et la commission scolaire de Yamaskaville, 1930-1960*, in: *Historical Studies in Education/Revue d'histoire de l'éducation*, 3:1 (1991), pp. 49-74.

DEL PILAR GUTIÉRREZ LORENZO, M., *La escuela para señoritas fundada por las hermanas de la Caridad en 1861: el primer plantel de maestras en Jalisco*, in: L.E. GALVÁN LAFARGA & O. LÓPEZ PÉREZ (eds.), *Entre imaginarios y Utopías: Historias de maestras*, México, CIESAS-UNAM-PUEG, 2008.

DEL VALLE LÓPEZ, A., *La actividad educadora, directa e institucional: órdenes y congregaciones femeninas dedicadas a la enseñanza*, in: B. BARTOLOMÉ MARTÍNEZ (ed.), *Historia de la acción educadora de la iglesia en España*, I: *Edades Antigua, Media y Moderna* (Biblioteca de autores cristianos. Series maior 49), Madrid, Biblioteca de Autores Cristianos, 1995, pp. 723-745.

— *La actividad educadora institucional: órdenes, congregaciones e institutos eclesiásticos femeninos dedicados a la educación enseñanza*, in: B. BARTOLOMÉ MARTÍNEZ (ed.), *Historia de la acción educadora de la iglesia en España, II: Edad Contemporánea* (Biblioteca de autores cristianos. Series maior 54), Madrid, Biblioteca de Autores Cristianos, 1997, pp. 512-718.

DE MAEYER, J., LEPLAE, S. & SCHMIEDL, J., *Religious Institutes in Western Europe in the 19th and 20th Centuries: An Underrated History*, in: J. DE MAEYER, S. LEPLAE & J. SCHMIEDL (eds.), *Religious Institutes in Western Europe in the 19th and 20th Centuries. Historiography, Research and Legal Position* (KADOC Studies on Religion, Culture & Society, 2), Leuven, Leuven University Press, 2004, pp. 7-26.

DE MAEYER, J., LEPLAE, S. & SCHMIEDL, J. (eds.), *Religious Institutes in Western Europe in the 19th and 20th Centuries. Historiography, Research and Legal Position* (KADOC Studies on Religion, Culture & Society, 2), Leuven, Leuven University Press, 2004.

DEPAEPE, M. et al., *Orde in vooruitgang: Alledaags handelen in de Belgische lagere school (1880-1970)* (Studia Paedagogica 25), Leuven, Universitaire Pers, 1999 [translation: *Order in Progress: Everyday Educational Practice in Primary Schools, Belgium, 1880-1970* (Studia paedagogica 29), Leuven, Leuven University Press, 2000].

DEPAEPE, M., DEBAERE, F. & VAN ROMPAEY, L., *Missionary Education in the Belgian Congo during the Colonial Period (1908-1960)*, in: *Neue Zeitschrift für Missionswissenschaft/Nouvelle Revue de science missionaire*, 48:4 (1992), pp. 265-280.

DEPAEPE, M., LAUWERS, H. & SIMON, F., *De feminisering van het leerkrachtencorps*, in: *Revue belge de philologie et d'histoire/Belgisch Tijdschrift voor Filologie en Geschiedenis*, 82:4 (2004), pp. 969-995.

DEPAEPE, M., LAUWERS, H. & SIMON, F., *The Feminization of the Teaching Profession in Belgium in the Nineteenth and Twentieth Centuries*, in: R. CORTINA & S. SAN ROMAN (eds.), *Women and Teaching. Global Perspectives on the Feminization of a Profession*, New York, Palgrave, 2006, pp. 155-183.

DEPAEPE, M., LAUWERS, H., SIMON, F., HELLINCKX B. & VAN ROMPAEY, L., *Mapa de la Feminización de la Enseñanza Primaria en Bélgica*, in: *Tempora: Revista de Sociología de la Educación*, 10 (2007), pp. 87-114.

DEPAEPE, M. & SIMON, F., *Is there any Place for the History of "Education" in the "History of Education"? A Plea for the History of Everyday Educational*

Reality in- and outside Schools, in: *Paedagogica Historica*, 31:1 (1995), pp. 9-16.

DEPAEPE, M. & VAN ROMPAEY, L., *In het teken van de bevoogding. De educatieve actie in Belgisch-Kongo 1908-1960*, Leuven, Garant, 1995.

DERKS, M., *Modesty and Excellence: Gender and Sports Culture in Dutch Catholic Schooling, 1900-40*, in: *Gender & History*, 20:1 (2008), pp. 8-26.

DERKS, M. & EIJT, J., *Wie kookte het laatste avondmaal? Over de zichtbaarheid van vrouwen in religiegeschiedenis*, in: M. ACKERMANS & T. HOOGBERGEN (eds.), *Kloosters en religieus leven: Historie en toekomst*, 's-Hertogenbosch, Heijnen, 2003, pp. 194-203.

DERKS, M. & VAN HEIJST, A., *Voor mensen, om God. De spirituele en sociale betekenis van vrouwelijke religieuzen in Nederland in de 19e en 20e eeuw*, forthcoming.

DERKS, M. & WOLF, R., *Wetenschap in dienstbaarheid: Ida B.M. Frye (1909), heilpedagoge* (Vrouwen van formaat, 2), Nijmegen, Vantilt, 2000.

DE SAINT MARTIN, M., *Une "bonne" éducation: Notre-Dame des Oiseaux à Sèvres*, in: *Ethnologie française*, 20:1 (1990), pp. 62-70.

DÉSILETS, A., *Gadbois, Albine, dite Marie de Bonsecours*, in: *Dictionary of Canadian Biography* (online).

DESMEULES, M., *Les communautés religieuses enseignantes*, in: *Saguenayensia* 44:2 (2002), pp. 27-35.

DE VIGUERIE, J., *Avant-Propos*, in: *Les religieuses enseignantes XVI - XX siècles. Actes de la quatrième rencontre d'histoire religieuse organisée à Fontevraud le 4 octobre 1980 par le Centre de Recherche d'Histoire Religieuse et d'Histoire des Idées (Université d'Angers) et le Centre Culturel de l'Ouest, Université d'Angers* (Publications du Centre de recherches d'histoire religieuse et d'histoire des idées 4), Angers, Presses de l'Université d'Angers, 1981, pp. 7-8.

DE VROEDE, M., *The Catholic Boarding Schools for Girls in Belgium before the First World War*, in: H. KANZ (ed.), *Bildungsgeschichte als Sozialgeschichte. Festschrift zum 60. Geburtstag von Franz Pöggeler*, (Erziehungsphilosophie 8), Frankfurt am Main, Peter Lang, 1986, pp. 313-337.

— *Religieuses et béguines enseignantes dans les Pays-Bas méridionaux et la Principauté de Liège aux XVIIe-XVIIIe siècles* (Studia Paedagogica 20), Leuven, Leuven University Press, 1996.

DE VROEDE, M., LORY, J. & SIMON, F., *Bibliographie de l'histoire de l'enseignement préscolaire, primaire, normal et spécial en Belgique 1774-1986*, Leuven, Acco, 1988.

DE WAELE, F., *Van Deugdsaeme Dogters en Vroome Meyskens. Pensionaatsopvoeding bij de Zusters van Liefde te Beerlegem 1823-1965*, Beerlegem, Mariaheem, 1985.

DOMPNIER, B. & FROESCHLÉ-CHOPARD, M.-H. (eds.), *Les religieux et leurs livres à l'époque moderne. Actes du colloque de Marseille, EHESS, 2 et 3 avril 1997* (Collection Histoires croisées), Clermont-Ferrand, Presses universitaires Blaise-Pascal, 2000.

DRAINVILLE, M., *Porteuses de vie en Amérique: Les Sœurs des Saints Cœurs de Jésus et de Marie depuis 1891*, Joliette, 2003.

DRIVER, E., *Culinary Landmarks. A Bibliography of Canadian Cookbooks, 1825-1949*, Toronto, University of Toronto Press, 2008.

DUFOUR, A., *Les manuels de "Connaissances scientifiques usuelles" des Soeurs de Sainte-Anne, 1923-1956*, in: M. LEBRUN (ed.), *Le manuel scolaire d'ici et d'ailleurs, d'hier à demain*, Québec, Presses de l'université du Québec, 2007.

DUMONT, M., *Des garderies au 19e siècle: les salles d'asile des Soeurs Grises à Montréal*, in: N. FAHMY-EID & M. DUMONT, *Maîtresses de maison, maîtresses d'école: femmes, famille et éducation dans l'histoire du Québec* (Études d'Histoire du Québec), Montreal, Boréal Express, 1983, pp. 261-285.

— *Une tradition de gestion féminine en éducation*, in: *La gestion de l'éducation au féminin. Colloque "La gestion de l'éducation au féminin"*, Chicoutimi, UQAC, 1986, pp. 7-21.

— *Le défi des religieuses enseignantes d'aujourd'hui*, in: *Canadian Woman Studies/ Les cahiers de la femme*, 7:3 (1986), pp. 51-54 (revised and enlarged version of an article which appeared in *AREQ, l'Association des religieuses enseignantes du Québec*, 23:1 (1983)).

— *Une perspective féministe dans l'histoire des congrégations de femmes*, in: *SCHEC Études d'histoire religieuse*, 57 (1990), pp. 29-35.

— *Girls' Schooling in Quebec: 1639-1960* (Historical Booklet No. 49), Ottawa, Canadian Historical Association, 1990.

— *Les religieuses sont-elles féministes?*, Montreal, Bellarmin, 1995.

— *Grandir au pensionnat au Québec au tournant des années 1950*, in: *Historical Studies in Education/Revue d'histoire de l'éducation*, 20:2 (2008), pp. 111-121.

DUMONT, M. & CHAMPAGNE, L., *Le financement des pensionnats de jeunes filles: le modèle de la congrégation des Sœurs de Sainte-Anne, 1850-1950*, in: *Société canadienne d'histoire de l'Église catholique (SCHEC) Sessions d'étude*, 53 (1986), pp. 63-91.

DUMONT, M. & FAHMY-EID, N. (eds.), *Les couventines: l'éducation des filles au Québec dans les congrégations religieuses enseignantes 1840-1960*, Montreal, Boréal, 1986.

DUMONT, M. & MALOUIN, M.-P., *Évolution et rôle des congrégations religieuses enseignantes féminines au Québec, 1840-1960*, in: *Société canadienne d'histoire de l'Église catholique (SCHEC) Sessions d'étude*, 50 (1983), pp. 201-230.

DURET, A., *Les communautés religieuses enseignantes et missionnaires à Luçon aux XVIIe-XVIIIe siècles*, Lille, A.N.R.T, Université de Lille III, 1996.

EIJT, J., *Van geestelijke moeders en jonge juffrouwen. Zusters in opvoeding en onderwijs*, in: M. VAN DER PLAS (ed.), *Kostschool...een les voor het leven?*, 's-Hertogenbosch, Het Noordbrabants Genootschap, 1991, pp. 55-76.

— *Verborgen vrouwen, vergeten vrouwen? Veranderende visies op de geschiedenis van negentiende-eeuwse zustercongregaties*, in: *Trajecta: tijdschrift voor de geschiedenis van het katholiek leven in de Nederlanden*, 1 (1992), pp. 374-387.

— *Zorgende zusters en hulpeloze zielen. De opvang van verlaten kinderen in 's-Hertogenbosch 1813-1900*, in: J.A.F.M. VAN OUDHEUSDEN, P.H.A.M. ABELS, J.G.M. BIEMANS & A.P.F. WOUTERS (eds.), *Ziel en zaligheid in Noord-Brabant*, Delft, Eburon, 1993, pp. 332-344.

— *"Daar was je dochter veilig". Vrouwelijke religieuzen en de zorg voor zwakzinnige meisjes, 1924-1955*, in: A. VAN HEIJST & M. DERKS (eds.), *Terra incognita. Historisch onderzoek naar katholicisme en vrouwelijkheid*, Kampen, Kok Agora, 1994, pp. 149-172.

— *Religieuze vrouwen. Bruid, moeder, zuster. Geschiedenis van twee Nederlandse zustercongregaties, 1820-1940*, Hilversum, Verloren, 1995.

— *"Het is hard werken geweest, dag en nacht." De Zusters van de Choorstraat en hun zorg voor zwakzinnige meisjes, 1924-1955*, in: *Brabants Heem* 48:3 (1996), pp. 103-111.

— *Zorgen in Gods naam. Ursulinen van Bergen 1898-1998*, Hilversum, Verloren, 1998.

— *Zuster Marie van Uden (1895-1975): Pionier in het buitengewoon onderwijs*, in: J. BROUWERS et al. (eds.), *Brabantse biografieën. Levensbeschrijvingen van bekende en onbekende Noord-Brabanders*, vol. 6, 's-Hertogenbosch, Stichting Brabantse Regionale Geschiedbeoefening, 2003.

EIJT, J. & HAUTVAST, S., *Een missie in de marge. Dochters van Onze Lieve Vrouw van het Heilig Hart in Nederland en Indonesië 1911-2000*, Hilversum, Verloren, 2002.

EIJT, J. & HILHORST, M., *"Een geïsoleerde opvoeding". Zusters en leerlingen op katholieke meisjespensionaten*, in: *"En Marie werd wijzer..." Culturele verschijningsvormen van meisjesonderwijs in heden en verleden*, Nijmegen, Vereniging Landelijk Overleg Vrouwengeschiedenis, 1989, pp. 71-84.

EISENMANN, L., *Reconsidering a Classic: Assessing the History of Women's Higher Education a Dozen Years after Barbara Solomon*, in: *Harvard Educational Review*, 67:4 (1997), pp. 689-717.

ESCOLANO, A. (ed.), *La cultura material de la escuela. En el centenario de la Junta para la Ampliación de Estudios, 1907-2007*, Berlanga de Duero, Soria CEINCE, 2007.

FAHMY-EID, N., *L'histoire de l'éducation des filles au Québec, la pointe de l'iceberg*, in: *Historical Studies in Education/Revue d'histoire de l'éducation*, 3:2 (1991), pp. 224-236.

FAUBELL ZAPATA, V., *Educación y órdenes y congregaciones religiosas en la España del siglo XX*, in: *Revista de educación*, 1 (2000), pp. 137-200.

FAUGERAS, M., *Les Sœurs de l'Instruction Chrétienne de Saint-Gildas-des-Bois au XIXe siècle*, in: *Les religieuses enseignantes XVI - XX siècles. Actes de la quatrième rencontre d'histoire religieuse organisée à Fontevraud le 4 octobre 1980 par le Centre de Recherche d'Histoire Religieuse et d'Histoire des Idées (Université d'Angers) et le Centre Culturel de l'Ouest, Université d'Angers* (Publications du Centre de recherches d'histoire religieuse et d'histoire des idées 4), Angers, Presses de l'Université d'Angers, 1981, pp. 101-113.

FERREIRA MELO, G. & INÁCIO FILHO, G., *Colégio Nossa Senhora Das Dores - Uberaba-Mg (1940-1966); Educação feminina*, in: *Revista HISTEDBR Online*, 15 (September 2004).

FERRETTI, L., *Histoire des Dominicaines de Trois-Rivières: "C'est à moi que vous l'avez fait"*, Sillery, Septentrion, 2002.

FITZGERALD, M., *The Perils of "Passion and Poverty": Women Religious and the Care of Single Women in New York City, 1845-1890*, in: *U.S. Catholic Historian*, 10:1-2 (1992) [= special issue *Women Religious: Historical Explorations*], pp. 45-58.

FITZPATRICK, T.A., *No Mean Achievement: Scottish Teacher Education 1895-1995*, Glasgow, Burns & Son, 1995.

FLAXMAN, R., *A Woman Styled Bold: the Life of Cornelia Connelly, 1809-1879*, London, Darton Longman & Todd, 1991.

FOALE, M.T., *The Josephite Story: The Sisters of St. Joseph: Their Foundation and Early History 1866-1893*, Sydney, St. Joseph's Generalate, 1989.

FOZ Y FOZ, P., *Las enseñanzas iberoamericanas: 1754-1820*, Bogotá, CELAM, 1988.

— *El convento de la enseñanza de México: ambivalencias de una joya de arte colonial*, Bogotá, CELAM, 1990.

— *Los monasterios de la enseñanza y la educación de la mujer en España e Iberoamérica*, in: M.I. VIFORCOS MARINAS & J. PANIAGUA PÉREZ (eds.), *I Congreso Internacional del Monacato Femenino en España, Portugal y America, 1492-1992*, vol. 1, León, Universidad de León - Servicio de Publicaciones, 1993, pp. 67-84.

— *Mujer y educación en Colombia Siglos XVI-XIX. Portaciones del Colegio de La Enseñanza, 1783-1900*, Santa fe de Bogotá, Academia Colombiana de Historia, 1997.

FRIEDRICH, M., « *Die Schülerinnen werden liebevoll behandelt - im Ganzen herrscht Zucht und Ordnung* »: *die Tätigkeit der weiblichen Schulorden in Salzburg*, in: I. BREHMER & G. SIMON (eds.), *Geschichte der Frauenbildung und Mädchenerziehung in Österreich*, Graz, Leykam, 1997, pp. 108-127.

FRITZER, E. (ed.), *300 Jahre Englische Fräulein in Österreich. Wegbereiterinnen moderner Frauenbildung*, Lienz, E. Fritzer, 2005.

GAGNON, A., *The Pensionnat Assomption: Religious Nationalism in a Franco-Albertan Boarding School for Girls, 1926-1960*, in: *Historical Studies in Education/Revue d'histoire de l'éducation*, 1:1 (1989), pp. 95-117.

GALE, F. (ed.), *Making Space: Women and Education at St Aloysius College 1880-2000*, Adelaide, Wakefield Press, 2000.

GALUSH, W.J., *What Should Janek Learn? Staffing and Curriculum in Polish-American Parochial Schools, 1870-1940*, in: *History of Education Quarterly*, 40:4 (2000), pp. 395-417.

GALVÁN LAFARGA, L.E. & LÓPEZ PÉREZ, O. (eds.), *Entre imaginarios y Utopías: Historias de maestras*, México, CIESAS-UNAM-PUEG, 2008.

GARCÍA GARGALLO, M., *L'ensenyament de l'església a la ciutat de Barcelona. Directori Estadístic*, PhD dissertation, University of Barcelona, 1999 (available online).

GARDINER, P., *An Extraordinary Australian: Mary MacKillop*, Alexandria, E J Dwyer in association with David Ell Press, 1994.

GATTI JÚNIOR, D. & DE M. OLIVEIRA, L.H.M., *Colégio Santa Teresa: um projeto Scalabriniano (1939-1942)*, in: *Revista HISTEDBR On-line*, 9 (March 2003).

GATTI JÚNIOR, D. & DE M. OLIVEIRA, L.H.M., *O Projeto Scalabriniano de Instrução Escolar: o Colégio Santa Teresa de Ituiutaba (1939-1942)*, in: *II Congresso de Pesquisa e Ensino em História da Educação em Minas Gerais, 2004, Uberlândia/MG. Anais do II Congresso de Pesquisa e Ensino em História da Educação em Minas Gerais*, vol. 1, Uberlândia, Editora da Universidade Federal de Uberlândia, 2003, pp. 815-825.

GATZ, E. (ed.), *Geschichte des Kirchlichen Lebens in den deutschsprachigen Ländern seit dem Ende des 18. Jahrhunderts: Die katholische Kirche, vol. 5: Caritas und soziale Dienste*, Freiburg, Herder, 1997.

— *Geschichte des kirchlichen Lebens in den deutschsprachigen Ländern seit dem Ende des 18. Jahrhunderts, vol. 7: Klöster und Ordensgemeinschaften*, Herder, Freiburg, 2006.

GEMIE, S., *Women and Schooling in France, 1815-1914. Gender, Authority and Identity in the Female Schooling Sector*, Keele, Keele University Press, 1995.

GERDES, M.R., *To Educate and Evangelize: Black Catholic Schools of the Oblate Sisters of Providence (1828-1880)*, in: *U.S. Catholic Historian*, 7:2-3 (1988), pp. 183-199.

GLASER, E. & SCHMID, P., *Biographieforschung in der Historischen Pädagogik*, in: H.-H. KRÜGER & W. MAROTZKI (eds.), *Handbuch erziehungswissenschaftliche Biographieforschung*, 2nd ed., Wiesbaden, Vs Verlag für Sozialw., 2006, pp. 363-389.

GLEASON, M., *Disciplining the Student Body: Schooling and the Construction of Canadian Children's Bodies, 1930–1960*, in: *History of Education Quarterly*, 41:2 (2001), pp. 189-215.

GOODSON, I. (ed.), *International Perspectives in Curriculum History*, London, Routledge, 1988.

GOOLEY MCPHERON, L.M., *A Historical Perspective of Career Patterns of Women in the Teaching Profession: 1900-1940*, PhD dissertation, Illinois State University, 1981.

GORDON, P. & ALDRICH, R., *Biographical Dictionary of North American and European Educationists*, London, The Woburn Press, 1997.

GORDON, P. & LAWTON, D., *Curriculum Change in the Nineteenth and Twentieth Centuries*, London, Hodder & Stoughton, 1978.

GOSSAGE, P., *Les enfants abandonées à Montréal au 19e siècle: la Crèche d'Youville des Soeurs Grises 1820-1871*, in: *Revue d'histoire de l'Amérique française*, 40:4 (1987), pp. 537-559.

GRACE, G., *Women Teachers as Organic Intellectuals*, in: *British Journal of Sociology of Education*, 16:3 (1995), pp. 415-417.

GRESKO, J., *The 'Serfs of the System'? Oblate Brothers and the Sisters of St. Ann in British Columbia Schools, 1858-1920*, in: *Western Oblate Studies/Études oblates de l'Ouest*, 4 (1996) [= R. HUEL (ed.), *Proceedings of the Fourth Symposium on the History of the Oblates in Western and Northern Canada/Actes du quatrième colloque sur l'histoire des Oblats dans l'Ouest et le Nord canadiens, 25-26 août/August 1995*], pp. 119-141.

GREW, R. & HARRIGAN, P.J., *The Catholic Contribution to Universal Schooling in France, 1850-1906*, in: *The Journal of Modern History*, 57:2 (1985), pp. 211-247.

GREW, R. & HARRIGAN, P.J., *School, State, and Society: The Growth of Elementary Schooling in Nineteenth-Century France – A Quantitative Analysis*, Ann Arbor, University of Michigan Press, 1991 [translation: *L'école primaire en France au 19e siècle: essai d'histoire quantitative* (Civilisations et sociétés 108), Paris, École des hautes études en sciences sociales, 2002].

GROSVENOR, I., LAWN, M. & ROUSMANIERE, K. (eds.), *Silences and Images: the Social History of the Classroom*, New York, Peter Lang, 1999.

GRUBER, E., *Erziehungs- und Bildungsarbeit der Franziskanerinnen von Sießen in der Zeit von 1854 bis 1940*, in: *Rottenburger Jahrbuch für Kirchengeschichte*, 14 (1995), pp. 153-176.

HALLMAN, D.M., *"Woman of Exodus II": Irene Poelzer, the Women's Movement, and Teacher Education*, in: STORTZ & PANAYOTIDIS, *Historical Identities*, pp. 225-247.

HALLMAN, D.M. & LATHROP, A.H., *Sustaining the Fire of "Scholarly Passion": Mary G. Hamilton (1883-1972) and Irene Poelzer (1926-)*, in: E.M. SMYTH &

P. BOURNE (eds.), *Women Teaching, Women Learning: Historical Perspectives*, Toronto, Inanna Publications & Education, 2006, pp. 45-64.

HAMEL, T., *Un siècle de formation des maîtres au Québec, 1836-1939* (Les Cahiers du Québec: collection "Psychopédagogie"), LaSalle, Éditions Hurtubise HMH ltée, 1995.

— *Les écoles normales au Québec: institutions d'Église ou d'État?*, in: J. COOLAHAN, R. ALDRICH & F. SIMON (eds.), *Faiths and Education: Historical and Comparative Perspectives* (*Paedagogica Historica* Supplementary Series 5), Gent, CSHP, 1999, pp. 193-215.

— *La production pédagogique des Sœurs de la Congrégation de Notre-Dame: 1858-1991*, in: *SCHEC Études d'histoire religieuse*, 65 (1999), pp. 67-87.

— *Teacher Training in Turmoil: The Experience of Professors in Normal Schools and Faculties of Education during the Quiet Revolution in Quebec*, in: P. STORTZ & E.L. PANAYOTIDIS (eds.), *Historical Identities: The Professoriate in Canada*, Toronto, University of Toronto Press, 2006, pp. 183-204.

HAMILTON, J., *The Nunnery as Menace: The Burning of the Charlestown Convent 1834*, in: *U.S. Catholic Historian*, 14:1 (1996) [= special issue *Beyond the Walls: Women Religious in American Life*], pp. 35-65.

HANOTEAU, M.-É., *Une grande Nivelloise. Mère Gertrude (Justine Desbille), fondatrice des Sœurs de l'Enfant-Jésus de Nivelles, 1801-1866*, Nivelles, Institut de l'Enfant-Jésus, 1985.

HARFORD, J., *The Movement for the Higher Education of Women in Ireland: Gender Equality or Denominational Rivalry?*, in: *History of Education*, 34:5 (2005), pp. 497-516.

— *An Experiment in the Development of Social Networks for Women: Women's Colleges in Ireland in the Nineteenth Century*, in: *Paedagogica Historica*, 43:3 (2007), pp. 365-381.

HARRIGAN, P.J., *The 'Histoire de l'éducation' and Canadian Historians*, in: *Historical Studies in Education/Revue d'histoire de l'éducation*, 3:2 (1991), pp. 269-273.

— *Women Teachers and the Schooling of Girls in France: Recent Historiographical Trends*, in: *French Historical Studies*, 21:4 (1998), pp. 593-610.

HARRINGTON, A.M., *Creating Community: Mary Frances Clarke and Her Companions*, Dubuque, Sisters of Charity BVM, 2004.

HARRINGTON, A. & MOYLAN, P. (eds.), *Mundelin Voices: The Women's College Experience 1930-1991*, Chicago, Loyola, 2001.

HARRISON, V.V., *Changing Habits: A Memoir of the Society of the Sacred Heart*, New York, Doubleday, 1988.

HAVELANGE, I., *Vingt ans de bibliographie d'histoire de l'éducation française (1979-1998)*, in: *Histoire de l'éducation*, 93 (2002), pp. 59-89.

HAYES, M., *The Founding Years of Trinity College Washington, D.C.: A Case Study in Christian Feminism*, in: *U.S. Catholic Historian*, 10:1-2 (1992) [= special issue *Women Religious: Historical Explorations*], pp. 79-86.

HÉBERT, J. & DE SÉGONZAC, M.-C. (eds.), *Javouhey Anne-Marie: Correspondance, 1798-1851*, 4 vols., Paris, Cerf, 1994.

HELLINCKX, B., DEPAEPE, M. & SIMON, F., *The Educational Work of Catholic Women Religious in the 19th and 20th Centuries. A Historiographical Survey*, in: *Revue d'histoire ecclésiastique*, 104:2 (2009), pp. 483-503 (forthcoming).

HELLINCKX, B., DEPAEPE, M. & SIMON, F., *Reflexiones historiográficas sobre la implicación de las religiosas católicas en la educación*, paper presented at the *15th International Congress of the Asociación de Historiadores Latinoamericanistas Europeos* (AHILA), Leiden, 2008, to be published in a volume on women teachers in Belgium and Mexico (L.E. GALVÁN LAFARGA & F. SIMON (eds.), México, CIESAS).

HERBST, J., *The History of Education: State of the Art*, in: *Paedagogica Historica*, 35 (1999), pp. 737-747.

HILHORST, M., *Op kostschool bij de nonnen 1920-1965*, in: M. GREVER et al. (eds.), *Vrouwendomein. Woongeschiedenis van vrouwen in Nederland* (Tipje van de sluier 4), Amsterdam, Uitgeverij Sua, 1986, pp. 108-122.

— *Pas à deux mes enfants! Meisjesvriendschappen en opvoeding op kloosterpensionaten, 1920-1965*, in: *Comenius. Wetenschappelijk tijdschrift voor de democratisering van opvoeding, onderwijs, vorming en hulpverlening*, 8:4 (1988), pp. 442-460.

— *Bij de zusters op kostschool. Geschiedenis van het dagelijks leven van meisjes op Rooms-katholieke pensionaten in Nederland en Vlaanderen*, Utrecht, Bruna, 1989.

— *Van jonge juffrouwen en kwekelingen. Katholieke meisjeskostscholen in de eerste helft van de twintigste eeuw*, in: M. GREVER & A. VAN DER VEEN (eds.), *Bij ons moeder en ons Jet. Brabantse vrouwen in de 19de en 20ste eeuw*, Zutphen, Walburgpers, 1989, pp. 100-121.

HOLMES, M. & WEISS, B.J., *Lives of Women Public Schoolteachers. Scenes from American Educational History*, New York, Garland Publishing, 1995.

HOY, S., *Review of C.K. Coburn & M. Smith, Spirited Lives: How Nuns Shaped Catholic Culture and American Life, 1836-1920 (Chapel Hill: University of North Carolina Press, 1999)*, in: *History of Education Quarterly*, 41:1 (2001), pp. 101-103.

— *No Color Line at Loretto Academy: Catholic Sisters and African Americans on Chicago's South Side*, in: *Journal of Women's History*, 14:1 (2002), pp. 8-33 (reprinted in S. HOY, *Good Hearts: Catholic Sisters in Chicago's Past*, Urbana, University of Illinois Press, 2006).

— *Good Hearts: Catholic Sisters in Chicago's Past*, Urbana, University of Illinois Press, 2006.

HUG, W., *Mädchenbildung als Auftrag der Frauenorden. Ein geschichtlicher Rückblick*, in: *Katholische Bildung*, 98:9 (1997), pp. 345-354.

HUNTLEY-MAYNARD, J., *Catholic Post-secondary Education for Women in Quebec: its Beginnings in 1908*, in: *Canadian Catholic Historical Association Historical Studies*, 59 (1992), pp. 37-48.

HUOT, G., *Un rêve inouï ... des milliers de jeunes. Mère Marie-Élisabeth (1840-1881), fondatrice de la Congrégation des Sœurs de Notre-Dame du Saint-Rosaire de Rimouski*, Sainte-Foy, Anne Sigier, 1991.

JACOB, L., *Loué sois-tu pour mes soeurs les saisons! Les Sœurs de Saint-François-d'Assise au Canada, 1904-2004*, Québec, 2004.

JACOBI, J., *Schoolmarm, Volkserzieher, Kantor und Schulschwester: German Teachers among German Immigrants during the Second Half of the Nineteenth Century*, in: H. GEITZ et al. (eds.), *German Influences on Education in the United States of America to 1917*, Washington/Cambridge, German Historical Institute/Cambridge University Press, 1995, pp. 115-128.

— *"Entzauberung der Welt" oder "Rettung der Welt". Mädchen- und Frauenbildung im 19. Jahrhundert in Deutschland*, in: *Zeitschrift für Erziehungswissenschaft*, 9:2 (2006), pp. 171-186.

KEALY, M., *Dominican Education in Ireland 1820-1930*, Dublin, Irish Academic Press, 2007.

KIENLE, P. & LUTZ-EFINGER, K., *Komm Schwester, tritt ins Licht. Schwester Philomena (Gertrud Schmittdiel), Generaloberin der Schwestern der Christlichen Liebe* (Glaube und Leben 17), Berlin, Lit-verlag, 2004.

KILLERBY, C.K., *Ursula Frayne: A Biography*, Fremantle, Fremantle Arts Centre Press, 1997.

KILROY, P., *Madeleine-Sophie Barat, 1779-1865: A Life*, New York, Paulist Press, 2000 [translation: *Madeleine Sophie Barat. Une vie (1779-1865)*, Paris, Cerf, 2004].

— *The Writing of Religious Women's History: Madeleine Sophie Barat (1779-1865)*, in: R. RAUGHTER (ed.), *Religious Women and their History: Breaking the Silence*, Dublin: Irish Academic Press, 2005, pp. 9-24.

KLARE, A., *Die Deutschen Heimschulen 1941-1945. Zur Gleichschaltung und Verstaatlichung kirchlicher, privater und stiftlicher Internatschulen im Nationalsozialismus*, in: *Jahrbuch für Historische Bildungsforschung*, 9 (2003), pp. 37-58.

KLUCHERT, G., *Biographie und Institution. Eine deutsches Gymnasium und seine Lehrer in verschiedenen politischen Systemen*, in: *Jahrbuch für Historische Bildungsforschung*, 12 (2006), pp. 9-36.

KOLLAR, R., *Foreign and Catholic: A Plea to Protestant Parents on the Dangers of Convent Education in Victorian England*, in: *History of Education*, 31:4 (2002), pp. 335-350.

— *Flowers, Pictures, and Crosses: Criticisms of Priscilla Lydia Sellon's Care of Young Girls*, in: *Anglican Theological Review*, 86 (2004), pp. 451-471.

KOLMER, E., *Catholic Women Religious and Women's History: A Survey of the Literature*, in: *American Quarterly*, 30:5 (1978) [= special Issue *Women and Religion*], pp. 639-651.

— *Women Religious in the United States: A Survey of Recent Literature*, in: C. KAUFFMAN (ed.), *Women Religious: Historical Explorations* (special issue of *U.S. Catholic Historian*, 10:1-2), New York, United States Catholic Historical Society, 1992, pp. 87-92.

KYLE, N., *Her Natural Destiny: The Education of Women in New South Wales*, Kensington, New South Wales University Press, 1986.

LABARRÈRE-PAULÉ, A., *L'instituteur laïque canadien français au 19ème siècle*, in: *Report of the Annual Meeting/Rapports annuels de la Société historique du Canada*, 42:1 (1963), pp. 102-115.

— *Les instituteurs laïques au Canada français, 1836-1900*, Quebec, Presses de l'Université Laval, 1965.

LACROIX, M.-T., *La vie à Saint-André au XIXème siècle (1796-1914)*, 2 vols., Tournai, ARSA, Religieuses de Saint-André, 2007.

LALOUETTE, J. & MACHELON, J-P. (eds.), *Les Congrégations hors-la-loi? Autour de la loi du 1er juillet 1901*, Paris, Cerf, 2002.

LAMIRANDE, É., *Elisabeth Bruyère, Fondatrice des Sœurs de la Charité d'Ottawa*, Montreal, Éditions Bellarmin, 1992.

LAMONTAGNE, E. & COHEN, Y., *Les Soeurs Grises à l'Université de Montréal, 1923-1947: de la gestion hospitalière à l'enseignement supérieur en nursing*, in: *Historical Studies in Education/Revue d'histoire de l'éducation*, 15:2 (2003), pp. 273-297.

LANCASTER, J., *Cornelia Connelly and her Interpreters*, Oxford, Way Books, 2004.

LANDY, T., *The Colleges in Context*, in: T. SCHIER & C. RUSSETT (eds.), *Catholic Women's Colleges in America*, Baltimore, The Johns Hopkins University Press, 2002, pp. 55-97.

LANFREY, A., *Sécularisation, séparation et guerre scolaire. Les catholiques français et l'école (1901-1914)*, Paris, Cerf, 2003.

LANGLOIS, C., *Review of Les religieuses enseignantes XVI - XX siècles (Angers: Presse de l'Université d'Angers, 1981)*, in: *Archives des sciences sociales des religions* 54:2 (1982), p. 195.

— *Le Catholicisme au féminin*, in: *Archives des sciences sociales des religions*, 57:1 (1984), pp. 29-53.

— *Le catholicisme au féminin. Les congrégations françaises à supérieure générale au XIXe siècle*, Paris, Cerf, 1984.

— *La fabrique des enseignantes. L'Église catholique, les femmes et l'école en France au XIXe siècle*, in: A. CROIX, A. LESPAGNOL & G. PROVOST (eds.), *Église, éducation, Lumières... Histoires culturelles de la France (1500-1830). En l'honneur de Jean Quéniart*, Rennes, Presses universitaires de Rennes, 1999, pp. 163-169.

LAPERLE, D., "*Une parole de Dieu fraîchement exprimée": fondements, usages et représentations du musée scolaire dans les pensionnats de filles des Soeurs des Saints Noms de Jésus et de Marie (1843-1981)*, in: *Historical Studies in Education/Revue d'histoire de l'éducation*, 19:1 (2007), pp. 53-79.

LAPERRIÈRE, G., *Table ronde: "L'historiographie des congrégations religieuses: approches actuelles"*, in: *SCHEC Études d'histoire religieuse*, 57 (1990), pp. 21-27.

— *Les communautés religieuses au Québec: pour une approche par familles spirituelles*, in: *SCHEC Études d'histoire religieuse*, 67 (2001), pp. 167-182.

— *Comment écrit-on l'histoire d'une communauté? Note critique*, in: *SCHEC Études d'histoire religieuse*, 71 (2005), pp. 101-110.

LAURIN, N. JUTEAU, D. & DUCHESNE, L., *À la recherche d'un monde oublié. Les communautés religieuses de femmes au Québec de 1900 à 1970*, Montreal, Le Jour, 1991.

LAWN, M. & GROSVENOR, I. (eds.), *Materialities of Schooling. Design, Technology, Objects, Routines*, Oxford, Symposium Books, 2005.

LEBRUN, M., *Un florilège moralisateur et nationaliste: le canon des études littéraires selon les manuels des communautés religieuses québécoises (1900-1950)*, in: *SCHEC Études d'histoire religieuse*, 71 (2005), pp. 33-50.

LECOMTE, L., *Architecture para-conventuelle: les pensionnats de l'ordre de la Visitation au XVIIIe siècle*, unpublished paper presented at the *5me Rencontre d'architecture européenne: Bâtiments Publiques II (Les écoles, les universités et les bâtiments des institutions sociales)*, Utrecht, 2008.

LECUIR-NEMO, G., *Anne-Marie Javouhey, fondatrice de la congrégation des soeurs de Saint-Joseph de Cluny (1779-1851)*, Paris, Karthala, 2001.

LE GOFF, Y., *Les Répercussions des laïcisations sur les activités des Soeurs de Saint-Joseph de Cluny*, in: *Archives de l'Église de France. Bulletin de l'Association des archivistes de l'Église de France*, 57 (2002), pp. 11-15.

LEI, C., *The Material Culture of the Loretto School for Girls in Hamilton, Ontario, 1865-1971*, in: *Canadian Catholic Historical Association Historical Studies*, 66 (2000), pp. 92-113.

— *"The Science Ball": Poetry as Historical Evidence*, in: *Canadian Catholic Historical Association Historical Studies*, 70 (2004), pp. 9-28.

LEJEUNE, P., *Les instituteurs du XIXe siècle racontent leur vie*, in: *Histoire de l'éducation*, 25 (1985), pp. 53-82.

— *Répertoire des autobiographies écrites en France au XIXe siècle: vies d'instituteurs*, in: *Histoire de l'éducation*, 25 (1985), pp. 83-104.

LEMARIÉ, C., *Les premières congrégations religieuses féminines aux États-Unis dans la première moitié du XIXe siècle*, in: *Les religieuses enseignantes XVI - XX siècles. Actes de la quatrième rencontre d'histoire religieuse organisée à Fontevraud le 4 octobre 1980 par le Centre de Recherche d'Histoire Religieuse et d'Histoire des Idées (Université d'Angers) et le Centre Culturel de l'Ouest, Université d'Angers* (Publications du Centre de recherches d'histoire religieuse et d'histoire des idées 4), Angers, Presses de l'Université d'Angers, 1981, pp. 137-150.

LEONARD, E., *Frances Taylor, Mother Magdalen SMG. A Portrait 1832-1900*, Roehampton, Maryfield Convent, 2005.

LESSARD, S., *"The Luxury of Order"*, in: *House Beautiful*, Dec. 1995, pp. 16-124.

LINEHAN, M., *"Nazareth College Leads the Way": Catholicism, Democracy, and Racial Justice at a Southern College, 1920-1955*, in: *U.S. Catholic Historian*, 19:1 (2001), pp. 65-77.

LLUÏSA CANUT, M. & LUIS AMORÓS, J., *Maestras y libros (1850-1912): La primera Normal femenina de Baleares*, Palma/Mao, Universitat de les Illes Balears/Institut Menorquí d'Estudis, 2000.

LOGAN, G. & WATSON, T. (eds.), *Soldiers of the Service: Some Early Queensland Educators and their Schools*, Brisbane, History of Queensland Education Society, 1992.

LONGSTREET, W.S. & SHANE, H.G., *Curriculum for a New Millennium*, Boston, Allyn and Bacon, 1993.

LUC, J.-N., *L'invention du jeune enfant. De la salle d'asile à l'école maternelle*, Paris, Belin, 1997.

LUIRARD, M., *Madeleine-Sophie Barat (1779-1865). Une éducatrice au coeur du monde*, Paris, Nouvelle Cité, 1999.

— *Les Dames du Sacré-Cœur*, in: J. LALOUETTE & J-P. MACHELON (eds.), *Les Congrégations hors-la-loi? Autour de la loi du 1er juillet 1901*, Paris, Cerf, 2002, pp. 257-270.

LUX-STERRITT, L., *Between the Cloister and the World: the Successful Compromise of the Ursulines of Toulouse, 1604-1616*, in: *French History*, 16:3, 2002, pp. 247-268.

— *Redefining Female Religious Life: French Ursulines and English Ladies in Seventeenth-Century Catholicism*, Aldershot, Ashgate, 2005.

MACCURTAIN, M., *Late in the Field: Catholic Sisters in Twentieth-Century Ireland and the New Religious History*, in: J. HOFF & M. COULTER (eds.), *Irish Women's Voices Past and Present* (special issue of *Journal of Women's*

History vols. 6-7), Bloomington (Ind.), Johns Hopkins University Press, 1995, pp. 49-63.

MACGINLEY, M.R., *A Dynamic of Hope: Institutes of Women Religious in Australia*, Sydney, Crossing Press, 1996.

MAGRAY, M.P., *The Transforming Power of the Nuns: Women, Religion, and Cultural Change in Ireland, 1750-1900*, New York, Oxford University Press, 1998.

MAIERHOFER, B., *Schulen der Disziplin hinter Klostermauern. Die Frauenschulorden in Graz im 19. und 20. Jahrhundert*, in: I. BREHMER & G. SIMON (eds.), *Geschichte der Frauenbildung und Mädchenerziehung in Österreich*, Graz, Leykam, 1997, pp. 141-161.

MAILLOUX, C., *Une femme dans la tourmente*, Lachine, Éditions Sainte-Anne, 1992.

MALOUIN, M.-P., *Les rapports entre l'école privée et l'école publique: l'académie Marie-Rose au 19e siècle*, in: N. FAHMY-EID & M. DUMONT, *Maîtresses de maison, maîtresses d'école: femmes, famille et éducation dans l'histoire du Québec* (Études d'Histoire du Québec), Montreal, Boréal Express, 1983, pp. 77-91, 381-382.

— *Ma soeur, à quelle école allez-vous? Deux écoles de filles à la fin du XIXème siècle*, Montreal, Fides, 1985.

— *Que sont devenues les sœurs de nos écoles? Recherche sur les orientations actuelles des religieuses enseignantes au Québec*, Sherbrooke, Association des religieuses enseignantes du Québec (AREQ), 1989.

— *La laïcisation de l'école publique québécoise entre 1939 et 1969: un processus de masculinisation*, in: *Historical Studies in Education/Revue d'histoire de l'éducation*, 4:1 (1992), pp. 1-29.

— *Les Congrégations féminines et la fondation des écoles normales de filles à Montréal*, in: E. TARDY et al., *Les bâtisseuses de la Cité* (Les Cahiers scientifiques 79), Montreal, ACFAS, 1993, pp. 141-148.

— *Review of C. AINSLEY, Eulalie Durocher (Laval: Méridien, 1993), C. MAILLOUX, Une femme dans la tourmente (Lachine: Sainte-Anne, 1992), A. MIGNEAULT, Cent ans d'espérance. Les Sœurs de l'Assomption de la Sainte Vierge dans l'Ouest canadien, 1891-1991 (Nicolet: S.A.S.V., 1991), L. ROY, Les Sœurs de Sainte-Anne, II (Montreal: Paulines et Soeurs de Sainte-Anne, 1992)*, in: *SCHEC Études d'histoire religieuse*, 60 (1994), pp. 141-146.

MANGION, C.M., *"Good Teacher" or "Good Religious"? The Professional Identity of Catholic Women Religious in Nineteenth-Century England and Wales*, in: *Women's History Review*, 14 (2005), pp. 223-239.

— *Contested Identities: Catholic Women Religious in Nineteenth-century England and Wales*, Manchester, Manchester University Press, 2008.

MARGADANT, J.B., *Madame le Professeur: Women Educators in the Third Republic*, Princeton, Princeton University Press, 1990.

MARQUESA DE RIO MAIOR, *Fundação da Ordem das Terceiras de S. Domingos em Portugal*, Lisboa, Irmãs Dominicanas de Santa Catarina de Sena, 1987.

MARTIN, J. & GOODMAN, J., *Women and Education 1800-1980. Educational Reform and Personal Identities*, Basingstoke, Palgrave Macmillan, 2004.

MARTIN, J. & GOODMAN, J., *Individual Lives and Social Histories*, in: J. MARTIN & J. GOODMAN, *Women and Education 1800-1980. Educational Reform and Personal Identities*, Basingstoke, Palgrave Macmillan, 2004, pp. 7-26.

MATTINGLY, C., *Uncovering Forgotten Habits: Anti-Catholic Rhetoric and Nineteenth-Century American Women's Literacy*, in: *College Composition and Communication*, 58:2 (2006), pp. 160-181.

MAURER, C., *Le catholicisme au féminin: l'expansion des congrégations dans l'Allemagne du XIXe siècle*, in: *Histoire, Economie et Société*, 21:1 (2002), pp. 17-28.

MAYEUR, F., *Vers un enseignement secondaire catholique des jeunes filles*, in: G. CHOLVY & N.-J. CHALINE (eds.), *L'enseignement catholique en France aux XIXe et XXe siècles. Actes du colloque organisé par la Société d'histoire religieuse de la France (Toulouse, 18-20 mars 1994) et de la journée d'étude de l'Association française d'histoire religieuse contemporaine (Paris, 24 septembre 1994)* (Histoire religieuse de la France 8), Paris, Cerf, 1995, pp. 197-205.

— *La formation des institutrices avant la loi Paul Bert. Les cours normaux*, in: G. CHOLVY & N.-J. CHALINE (eds.), *L'enseignement catholique en France aux XIXe et XXe siècles. Actes du colloque organisé par la Société d'histoire religieuse de la France (Toulouse, 18-20 mars 1994) et de la journée d'étude de l'Association française d'histoire religieuse contemporaine (Paris, 24 septembre 1994)* (Histoire religieuse de la France 8), Paris, Cerf, 1995, pp. 121-130.

— *L'éducation des filles vue par l'Église catholique au début du XIXe siècle*, in: G. LEDUC (ed.), *L'éducation des femmes en Europe et en Amérique du Nord de la Renaissance à 1848: réalités et représentations* (Collection 'Des idées et des femmes'), Paris, L'Harmattan, 1997, pp. 442-450.

MCCARTHY, M., *Memories of a Catholic Girlhood*, San Diego, Harcourt Brace, 1974.

MCCLELLAND, V.A., *Review of C. Dyhouse, Girls Growing Up in Late Victorian and Edwardian England (London/Boston: Routledge/Kegan Paul, 1981) and A. Digby & P. Searby, Children, School and Society in Nineteenth Century Engeland (London/Basingstoke: Macmillan, 1981)*, in: *Victorian Studies*, 27:1 (1983), pp. 106-108.

MCDOUGALL, R., *Cornelia Connelly: Woman of Mercy and Educator*, in: *Records of the American Catholic Historical Society of Philadelphia* 107:1-2 (1996), pp. 45-65.

— *Cornelia Connelly's Innovations in Female Education, 1846-1864. Revolutionizing the School Curriculum for Girls*, Lewiston, Edwin Mellen Press, 2008.

MCGAHAN, E.W., *The Sisters of Charity of the Immaculate Conception: A Canadian Case Study*, in: *Canadian Catholic Historical Association Historical Studies*, 61 (1995), pp. 99-133.

MCGRATH, M.S., *These Women? Women Religious in the History of Australia: the Sisters of Mercy, Parramatta 1888-1988*, Kensington, New South Wales University Press, 1988.

MCGUIRE, R., *The Grey Sisters in the Red River Settlement, 1844-1870*, in: *Canadian Catholic Historical Association Historical Studies*, 53 (1986), pp. 21-37.

MCLAUGHLIN, D., *The Founding of the Irish Christian Brothers: Navigating the Realities through the Myths*, in: *Australian Ejournal of Theology* August 2005, Issue 5.

MCLAY, A., *Women Out of Their Sphere: A History of the Sisters of Mercy in Western Australia*, Northbridge, W.A. Vanguard Press, 1992.

— *Women on the Move: Mercy's Triple Spiral. A History of the Adelaide Sisters of Mercy, Ireland to Argentina 1856-1880 to South Australia 1880*, Adelaide, Sisters of Mercy, 1996.

MCNERGNEY VINYARD, J., *For Faith and Fortune: The Education of Catholic Immigrants in Detroit, 1805-1925*, Urbana, University of Illinois Press, 1998.

MEIWES, R., *Arbeiterinnen des Herrn: katholische Frauenkongregationen im 19. Jahrhundert* (Geschichte und Geschlechter 30), Frankfurt, Campus, 2000.

MEYER, J.-C., *La congrégation de Notre-Dame de la Compassion*, in: G. CHOLVY & N.-J. CHALINE (eds.), *L'enseignement catholique en France aux XIXe et XXe siècles. Actes du colloque organisé par la Société d'histoire religieuse de la France (Toulouse, 18-20 mars 1994) et de la journée d'étude de l'Association française d'histoire religieuse contemporaine (Paris, 24 septembre 1994)* (Histoire religieuse de la France 8), Paris, Cerf, 1995, pp. 131-144.

MIDDLETON, S., *Schooling and Radicalisation: Life Histories of New Zealand Feminist Teachers*, in: *British Journal of Sociology of Education*, 8:2 (1987), pp. 169-189 (reprinted in: L. STONE (ed.), *The Education Feminism Reader*, London, Routledge, 1994).

MINNS, H., *Catherine McAuley and the Education of Irish Roman Catholic Children in the Mid-Nineteenth Century*, in: M. HILTON & P. HIRSCH (eds.), *Practical Visionaries: Women, Education and Social Progress, 1790-1930*, Harlow, Longman, 2000, pp. 52-65.

MINTEN, L., *"De besten onder de goeden": 175 jaar zusters der Christelijke Scholen Vorselaar*, in: *Basis: Ledenblad van het COV*, 103:11 (8 juni 1996), pp. 40-41.

MISNER, B., *"Highly Respectable and Accomplished Ladies": Catholic Women Religious in America 1790-1850*, New York/London, Garland, 1988.

MITRANO, T., *Mother Joseph Butler*, in: M. SELLER, *Women Educators in the United States, 1820-1993: a Bio-bibliographical Sourcebook*, Westport, Greenwood Press, 1994.

MÖLLER, L., *Höhere Mädchenschulen in der Kurpfalz und im fränkischen Raum im 18. Jahrhundert* (Mainzer Studien zur Neueren Geschichte 5), Frankfurt am Main, Peter Lang 2001.

MOLETTE, C., *Conclusions*, in: *Les religieuses enseignantes XVI - XX siècles. Actes de la quatrième rencontre d'histoire religieuse organisée à Fontevraud le 4 octobre 1980 par le Centre de Recherche d'Histoire Religieuse et d'Histoire des Idées (Université d'Angers) et le Centre Culturel de l'Ouest, Université d'Angers* (Publications du Centre de recherches d'histoire religieuse et d'histoire des idées 4), Angers, Presses de l'Université d'Angers, 1981, pp. 151-162.

MONTEIRO, M., *Vroomheid in veelvoud. Geschiedenis van de Franciscanessen van Oirschot 1797-1997*, Hilversum, Verloren, 2000.

MORROW, D.B., *Persons of Color and Religious at the Same Time: The Oblate Sisters of Providence, 1828-1860*, Chapel Hill/London, University of North Carolina Press, 2002.

MOULINET, D., *Les publications françaises relatives à l'histoire des congrégations religieuses*, in: J. DE MAEYER, S. LEPLAE & J. SCHMIEDL (eds.), *Religious Institutes in Western Europe in the 19th and 20th Centuries. Historiography, Research and Legal Position* (KADOC Studies on Religion, Culture & Society, 2), Leuven, Leuven University Press, 2004, pp. 53-70.

MUNRO, P., *Subject to Fiction: Women Teachers' Life History Narratives and the Cultural Politics of Resistance*, Buckingham, Open University Press, 1998.

MURPHY, R., *Julie Billiart, Woman of Courage: The Story of the Foundress of the Sisters of Notre Dame*, New York, Paulist Press, 1995.

NORMAN, M., *Making a Path by Walking. Loretto Pioneers Facing the Challenges of Catholic Education on the North American Frontier*, in: *Canadian Catholic Historical Association Historical Studies*, 65 (1999), pp. 92-106.

NORTHEY, H., *St. Mary's Convent Schools*, in: B. DICKEY (ed.), *William Shakespeare's Adelaide 1860-1930*, Adelaide, South Australian Association of Professional Historians, 1992.

OATES, M.J., *"The Good Sisters": The Work and Position of Catholic Churchwomen in Boston, 1870-1940*, in: R.E. SULLIVAN & J.M. O'TOOLE (eds.), *Catholic Boston. Studies in Religion and Community 1870-1970*, Boston, Roman Catholic Archbishop of Boston, 1985, pp. 171-200.

— *Mother Mary Regis Casserly*, in: M. SELLER, *Women Educators in the United States, 1820-1993: a Bio-bibliographical Sourcebook*, Westport, Greenwood Press, 1994.

— *Mother Mary Katharine Drexel*, in: M. SELLER, *Women Educators in the United States, 1820-1993: a Bio-bibliographical Sourcebook*, Westport, Greenwood Press, 1994.

— *Catholic Female Academies on the Frontier*, in: *U.S. Catholic Historian*, 12:4 (1994), pp. 121-136.

O'BRIEN, A., *God's Willing Workers: Women and Religion in Australia*, Sydney, University of New South Wales Press, 2005.

O'BRIEN, S., *"Terra incognita": The Nun in Nineteenth-century England*, in: *Past and Present*, 121 (1988), pp. 110-140.

— *A Survey of Research and Writing about Roman Catholic Women's Congregations in Great Britain and Ireland (1800-1950)*, in: J. DE MAEYER, S. LEPLAE & J. SCHMIEDL (eds.), *Religious Institutes in Western Europe in the 19th and 20th Centuries. Historiography, Research and Legal Position* (KADOC Studies on Religion, Culture & Society, 2), Leuven, Leuven University Press, 2004, pp. 91-116.

O'DONOGHUE, T.A., *Upholding the Faith: The Process of Education in Catholic Schools in Australia 1922-1965*, New York, Peter Lang, 2001.

— *Child-abuse Scandals and the Catholic Church: Are We Asking the Right Historical Questions?*, in: *History of Education Review*, 32:1 (2003), pp. 1-15.

— *Come Follow Me and Forsake Temptation: The Recruitment and Retention of Members of Catholic Teaching Orders, 1922-1965*, Bern, Lang, 2004.

— *Review of C. TRIMINGHAM JACK, Growing Good Catholic Girls: Education and Convent Life in Australia (Melbourne: Melbourne University Press, 2003)*, in: *History of Education Quarterly*, 45:3 (2005), pp. 493-495.

O'DONOGHUE, T. & BURLEY, S., *God's Antipodean Teaching Force: An Historical Exposition on Catholic Teaching Religious in Australia*, in: *Teaching and Teacher Education*, 24 (2008), pp. 180-189.

O'DONOGHUE, T. & POTTS, A., *Researching the Lives of Catholic Teachers who were Members of Religious Orders: Historiographical Considerations*, in: *History of Education*, 33:4 (2004), pp. 469-481.

O'FARRELL, M.P., *Nano Nagle, Woman of the Gospel*, Cork, Cork Publishing, 1996.

O'HAGAN, F.J., *The Contribution of the Religious Orders to Education in Glasgow during the Period 1847-1918*, Lampeter, Edwin Mellen Press, 2006.

OLDENHOF, H.J., *Van Normaalschool Steenwijkerwold naar Pabo Zwolle*, Zwolle, Pabo, 1987.

OSTROWITZKI, A., *Höhere Mädchenbildung bei den "Benediktinerinnen von der Ewigen Anbetung" in Bonn. Ein konfessioneller Streitfall im Vorfeld des*

Kulturkampfes, in: *Studien und Mitteilungen zur Geschichte des Benediktiner Ordens und seiner Zweige*, 113 (2002), pp. 501-513.
OURY, G.-M., *Les Ursulines de Québec 1639-1953*, Sillery, Septentrion, 1999.
PAISANT, C., *Les Soeurs de Picpus en Amérique latine: les premières missions d'éducation*, in: *Transversalités. Revue de l'Institut catholique de Paris*, 71 (1999), pp. 205-228.
PENEFF, J., *Autobiographies d'enseignants d'écoles publiques et privées*, in: *Les Cahiers du L.E.R.S.C.O.* 8 (January 1987).
PEREIRA DA SILVA ROSSI, M. & INÁCIO FILHO, G., *As congregações Católicas e a disseminação de escolas femininas no Triângulo Mineiro E Alto Paranaíba*, in: *Revista HISTEDBR On-line*, 24 (2006), pp. 79-92.
PERKO, F.M., *Religious Schooling in America: An Historiographical Reflection*, in: *History of Education Quarterly*, 40:3 (2000), pp. 320-338.
PERLMANN, J. & MARGO, R.A., *Women's Work? American Schoolteachers, 1650-1920*, Chicago, University of Chicago Press, 2001.
PÉRON, M., *Répercussions de la législation scolaire française (fin XIXe siècle début XXe siècle) sur la vie d'une congrégation bretonne: L'Immaculée*, in: *Archives de l'Église de France*, 56 (2001), pp. 15-22 & 57 (2001), pp. 13-24.
PERRONE, F.H., *"To Save them from the Dangers to their Faith": Documenting Student Life at Catholic Women's Colleges*, in: *Journal of Archival Organization*, 1:2 (2002), pp. 65-76.
PETERSON, C. & VAUGHN-ROBERSON, C.A., *Women with Vision: The Presentation Sisters of South Dakota, 1880-1985*, Urbana, University of Illinois Press, 1988.
PRENTICE, A. & THEOBALD, M.R., *The Historiography of Women Teachers: A Retrospect*, in: A. PRENTICE & M.R. THEOBALD (eds.), *Women who Taught: Perspectives on the History of Women and Teaching*, Toronto, University of Toronto Press, 1991, pp. 3-33.
PRENTICE, A. & THEOBALD, M.R. (eds.), *Women who Taught: Perspectives on the History of Women and Teaching*, Toronto, University of Toronto Press, 1991.
PUGA, A.-M., *Histoire de la Congrégation du Saint-Nom de Jésus de Toulouse: de 1800 à 1953*, Toulouse, Privat, 2006.
QUARTARARO, A.T., *Women Teachers and Popular Education in Nineteenth-Century France. Social Values and Corporate Identity at the Normal School Institution*, Newark, University of Delaware Press, 1995.
QUERTON, I., *La formation et la vie spirituelle des institutrices à l'école normale de l'Enfant Jésus (Nivelles) aux XIXe siècle*, in: *Revue d'histoire religieuse du Brabant wallon*, 2 (1988), pp. 288-289.
— *La préparation des institutrices à l'Institut de l'Enfant-Jésus (Nivelles) au 19e siècle: une formation totale de la personnalité*, in: L. COURTOIS & J. PIROTTE

(eds.), *Foi, gestes et institutions religieuses aux 19e et 20e siècles* (Collection Cerfaux-Lefort 9), Louvain-la-Neuve, UCL Centre d'histoire des religions, 1991, pp. 109-115.

RAFTERY, D. & KILBRIDE, C., *Reading the Image and Hearing the Voice: Using Technologies to Record and Interpret the Role of Catholic Religious Orders in Education and Literacy Formation*, unpublished paper presented at *ISCHE 28: Technologies of the Word. Literacies in the History of Education*, Umeå, Sweden, 16-19 August, 2006.

RAFTERY, D. & NOWLAN-ROEBUCK, C., *Convent Schools and National Education in Nineteenth-Century Ireland: Negotiating a Place within a Non-Denominational System*, in: *History of Education*, 36:3 (2007), pp. 353-365.

RAFTERY, D. & PARKES, S.M., *Female Education in Ireland 1700-1900: Minerva or Madonna*, Ontario, London and Dublin, Frank Cass/Irish Academic Press, 2007.

RAICHE, A. & BIERMAIER, A.M., *They Came to Teach: The Story of Sisters who Taught in Parochial Schools and their Contribution to Elementary Education in Minnesota*, St. Cloud, North Star Press, 1994.

RAPLEY, E., *A Social History of the Cloister: Daily Life in the Teaching Monasteries of the Old Regime*, Montreal, McGill-Queen's University Press, 2001.

RAUGHTER, R., *Pious Occupations: Female Activism and the Catholic Revival in Eighteenth-Century Ireland*, in: R. RAUGHTER (ed.), *Religious Women and their History: Breaking the Silence*, Dublin: Irish Academic Press, 2005.

RECKER, J.A.M., *Françoise Blin De Bourdon, Woman of Influence: The Story of the Cofoundress of the Sisters of Notre Dame*, New York, Paulist Press, 2001.

— *"Très affectueusement, votre mère en Dieu". Françoise Blin – French Aristocrat, Belgian Citizen, Co-Foundress of the Sisters of Notre Dame de Namur (1756-1838)* (Belgian Francophone Library 6), New York, Peter Lang, 2001.

REGAN, M., *Sister Jillian Havey*, in: P. DUIGNAN & D. GURR (eds.), *Leading Australia's Schools*, Sydney, ACEL and DEST, 2007.

RHÉAUME, C., *La création musicale chez les religieuses enseignantes de Montréal*, in: *Les Cahiers de l'ARMuQ* [*Association pour l'avancement de la recherche en musique du Québec*], 10 (June 1988), pp. 34-40.

RIBEIRO DE CASTRO, H., *Teresa de Saldanha – um projecto inovador no século XIX; uma interrogação para o século XXI*, in: M. FERNANDES, J.A. GONÇALVES, M. BOLINA, T. SALVADO & T. VITORINO (eds.), *O particular e o global no virar do milénio: cruzar saberes em educação. Actas do 5º congresso da sociedade portuguesa de ciências da educação*, Porto, Edições Colibri/SPCE, 2002, pp. 539-547.

— *A Portuguese School in the 19th Century: Reconstructing Life from Dead Documents*, paper presented at the *European Conference on Educational Research*,

University of Hamburg, 17-20 September, 2003 (available on Education-*line*).

— *The role of feminine civic societies and religious congregations in the history of educational and social change: A Portuguese case*, unpublished paper presented at *The European Conference on Educational Research (ECER) 2008: From Teaching to Learning?*, Göteborg, 11 September, 2008.

— *Teresa de Saldanha: Um projecto pedagógico inovador no século XIX, uma interrogação para o século XXI*, PhD dissertation, University of Lisbon, 2008.

— *Difusão da Cultura e Promoção da Vida: uma escola no centro de um bairro pobre na Lisboa do século XIX*, in: *Actas do V Congresso Luso-Brasileiro de História da Educação*, Évora, Universidade de Évora, forthcoming.

RINK, D., *Spirited Women: A History of Catholic Sisters in British Columbia*, Vancouver, Sisters Association of Vancouver Archdiocese, 2000.

ROBENSTINE, C., *French Colonial Policy and the Education of Women and Minorities: Louisiana in the Early Eighteenth Century*, in: *History of Education Quarterly*, 32:2, (1992), pp. 193-211.

ROGERS, R., *Reconsidering the Role of Religious Orders in Modern French Women's Education*, in: *Vitae Scholasticae*, 10:1-2 (1991), pp. 43-51.

— *Les demoiselles de la Légion d'honneur*, Paris, Plon, 1992.

— *Boarding Schools, Women Teachers, and Domesticity: Reforming Girls' Secondary Education in the First Half of the Nineteenth Century*, in: *French Historical Studies*, 19:1 (1995), pp. 153-181.

— *Retrograde or Modern? Unveiling the Teaching Nun in Nineteenth-century France*, in: *Social History*, 23:2 (1998), pp. 146-164.

— *Constructing French Womanhood over the Seas: Religious Teaching Congregations and the Civilizing Mission in Africa and the United States in the Nineteenth Century*, paper presented at the *XIXe Congrès international des sciences historiques*, Oslo, 2000 (available online).

— *Review of M. Hequet (ed.), L'éducation des filles au temps de George Sand (Arras: Artois Presses université, 1998)*, in: *CLIO, Histoire, Femmes et Sociétés*, 11 (2000) [= *Parler, chanter, lire, écrire*], online.

— *La sous-maîtresse française au XIXe siècle: domestique ou enseignante stagiaire?*, in: *Histoire de l'éducation*, 98 (2003), pp. 37-60.

— *Questioning National Models: The History of Women Teachers in a Comparative Perspective*, paper presented at the *20th International Congress of Historical Sciences - Women's History Revisited: Historiographical Reflections on Women and Gender in a Global Context*, University of New South Wales, Sydney, Australia, 8-9 July, 2005 (available online).

— *From the Salon to the Schoolroom: Educating Bourgeois Girls in Nineteenth-Century France*, University Park, Pennsylvania State University Press, 2005 [translation: *Les bourgeoises au pensionnat: L'éducation féminine au XIXe siècle*, Rennes, Presses universitaires de Rennes, 2007].

— *L'éducation des filles: un siècle et demi d'historiographie*, in: P. CASPARD, J.-N. LUC & R. ROGERS (eds.), *L'éducation des filles XVIIIe-XXIe siècles. Hommage à Françoise Mayeur*, special issue of *Histoire de l'éducation*, vol. 115-116 (2007), pp. 37-79.

— *Les enseignantes religieuses et laïques au XIXe siècle: vocation ou activité professionnelle*, in: J.-Y. CAUSER, R. PFEFFERKORN & B. WOEHL, *Métiers, identités professionnelles et genre*, Paris, L'Harmattan, 2007, pp. 33-50.

— *La place de la religion dans la formation des enseignantes religieuses et laïques en France avant 1880*, unpublished paper presented at the *Journée d'études 'Religion, fait religieux et laïcité dans la formation des enseignants (XVIe-XXe siècles)'*, Lille, 14 November, 2008.

ROGIER, N., *Zuster Maria Luykx (1904-1996): Oprichtster van Talenpracticum Regina Coeli*, in: P. TIMMERMANS et al. (eds.), *Brabantse biografieën. Levensbeschrijvingen van bekende en onbekende Noord-Brabanders*, vol. 5, 's-Hertogenbosch, Stichting Brabantse Regionale Geschiedbeoefening, 1999.

ROSS, S., *Faithful Companions of Jesus in the Field of Education in Brandon, Manitoba, 1883-1895*, in: *Canadian Catholic Historical Association Historical Studies*, 71 (2005), pp. 79-93.

ROUX, J., *L'enseignement primaire dans l'Ardèche sous la Monarchie de Juillet. La contribution des congrégations religieuses à l'enseignement élémentaire*, in: *Revue du Vivarais*, 94 (1993), pp. 125-142.

ROY, L., *Les pensionnats des Soeurs de Sainte-Anne dans la région métropolitaine 1850-1988*, in: *Cahiers de la Société historique de Montréal*, 7:1 (1988), pp. 364-372.

— *The Sisters of Saint Ann: A Century of History, 1900-1950*, vol. 2, Lachine, Les éditions Sainte-Anne, 1994.

RUBERG, W., *Children's Correspondence as a Pedagogical Tool in the Netherlands (1770-1850)*, in: *Paedagogica Historica*, 41:3 (2005), pp. 295-312.

RURY, J.L., *Education and Women's Work. Female Schooling and the Division of Labor in Urban America, 1870-1930*, Albany, State University of New York Press, 1991.

RUTZ, A., *Bildung - Konfession - Geschlecht. Religiöse Frauengemeinschaften und die katholische Mädchenbildung im Rheinland (16. - 18. Jahrhundert)*, Mainz, von Zabern, 2006.

SAEZ ISERN, F., *Congregaciones religiosas dedicadas a la enseñanza en Mallorca, 1794-1915*, in: *Mayurqa* 21 (1985-1987), pp. 279-288.

SAFIAN, J., *Educating the Heart and Mind: A History of Marymount School, 1926-2001*, New York, Marymount School, 2002.

SAINT-PIERRE, R. & WARD, Y., *Histoire des Soeurs de la Charité de Québec*, volume III: *Plus de cent cinquante ans d'histoire (1849-2001)*, Beauport, Publications MNH, 2003.

SAN ROMÁN GAGO, S., *La incorporación de la maestra a la escuela pública en España 1783-1882*, Cuadernos del Centro, México, El Colegio de San Luis, 2001.

SAVOIE, P. BRUTER, A. & FRIJHOFF, W., *Secondary Education: Institutional, Cultural and Social History*, in: *Paedagogica Historica*, 40:1-2 (2004), pp. 9-14.

SCHAFFER, W., *Schulorden im Rheinland: ein Beitrag zur Geschichte religiöser Genossenschaften im Erzbistum Köln zwischen 1815 und 1875* (Kölner Schriften zu Geschichte und Kultur 13), Köln, DME-Verlag, 1988.

SCHIER, T. & RUSSETT, C. (eds.), *Catholic Women's Colleges in America*, Baltimore, The Johns Hopkins University Press, 2002.

SCHILLINGER-PRASSL, C., *"Die jungen Fräulein in allen guten Sitten und Tugenden zu unterweisen". Die weiblichen Schulorden in Österreich in der Frühen Neuzeit*, in: I. BREHMER & G. SIMON (eds.), *Geschichte der Frauenbildung und Mädchenerziehung in Österreich*, Graz, Leykam, 1997, pp. 92-102.

SCHWEGMAN, M., *De strijd tegen de "mannelijke" blik. Vrouwengeschiedenis als eindexamenonderwerp*, in: *Tijdschrift voor Vrouwenstudies*, 11:2 (1990), pp. 184-196.

SEGERS, Y., DUJARDIN, C., KWANTEN, G., QUAGHEBEUR, P. & DE MAEYER, J., *150 Jaar Zusters van het Heilig Hart van Maria van Berlaar. In eenvoud en dienstbaarheid. 1845-1995*, Leuven, Zusters van het Heilig Hart van Maria, Berlaar & KADOC, 1995.

SÉGUY, J., *Review of C. LANGLOIS, Le catholicisme au féminin. Les congrégations françaises à supérieure générale au XIXe siècle (Paris: Cerf, 1984)*, in: *Archives des sciences sociales des religions*, 59:2 (1985), p. 275.

SELLER, M., *Women Educators in the United States, 1820-1993: a Bio-bibliographical Sourcebook*, Westport, Greenwood Press, 1994.

SHELDON, K., *"I Studied with the Nuns, Learning to Make Blouses": Gender Ideology and Colonial Education in Mozambique*, in: *The International Journal of African Historical Studies*, 31:3 (1998), pp. 595-625.

SICARD, G., *L'offensive de laïcisation de 1870-1871*, in: G. CHOLVY & N.-J. CHALINE (eds.), *L'enseignement catholique en France aux XIXe et XXe siècles. Actes du colloque organisé par la Société d'histoire religieuse de la France (Toulouse, 18-20 mars 1994) et de la journée d'étude de l'Association française d'histoire religieuse contemporaine (Paris, 24 septembre 1994)* (Histoire religieuse de la France 8), Paris, Cerf, 1995, pp. 35-46.

SIGMUND, B.B., *Sanctuary or prison? Review of V.V. HARRISON, Changing Habits: A Memoir of the Society of the Sacred Heart (New York: Doubleday, 1988)*, in: *The New York Times*, May 7, 1989.

SILVER, H., *Knowing and not Knowing in the History of Education*, in: *History of Education*, 21:1 (1992), pp. 97- 108.

SILVIA BASTOS, M.J., *Mulheres na sala de aula*, in: *Revista HISTEDBR On-line*, 21 (March 2006), pp. 15-25.

SIMON, F., *De produktie van schoolgedenkboeken (1977-1982). Weinig gelegenheid tot gejubel*, in: *Persoon en gemeenschap*, 35:7 (1982-1983), pp. 314-321.

SMYTH, E.M., *The Lessons of Religion and Science: the Congregation of the Sisters of St. Joseph and St. Joseph's Academy, Toronto, 1854-1911*, unpublished PhD dissertation, University of Toronto, 1990.

— *"A Noble Proof of Excellence": The Culture and Curriculum of a Nineteenth-Century Ontario Convent Academy*, in: R. HEAP & A. PRENTICE (eds.), *Gender and Education in Ontario: An Historical Reader*, Toronto, Canadian Scholars' Press, 1991, pp. 269-290.

— *Congregavit nos in unum Christi amor: The Congregation of the Sisters of St. Joseph, in the Archdiocese of Toronto, 1851-1920*, in: *Ontario History* 84:3 (1992), pp. 225-240.

— *"Developing the Powers of the Youthful Mind": The Evolution of Education for Young Women at St. Joseph's Academy, Toronto, 1854-1911*, in: *Canadian Catholic Historical Association Historical Studies*, 60 (1993-1994), pp. 103-125.

— *"Much Exertion of the Voice and Great Application of the Mind". Teacher Education within the Congregation of the Sisters of St. Joseph of Toronto, Canada, 1851-1920*, in: *Historical Studies in Education/Revue d'histoire de l'éducation*, 6:3 (1994), pp. 97-113.

— *Professionalization among the Professed: The Case of Roman Catholic Women Religious*, in: E.M. SMYTH, A. PRENTICE, S. ACKER & P. BOURNE (eds.), *Challenging Professions: Women and the Professions in English Canada*, Toronto, University of Toronto Press, 1999, pp. 234-254.

— *Writing the History of Women Religious in Canada (1996-2001)*, in: *International Journal of Canadian Studies/Revue internationale d'études canadiennes*, 23 (2001), pp. 207-213.

— *Preserving Habits: Memory within Communities of English Canadian Women Religious*, in: S.A. COOK, L.R. MCLEAN & K. O'ROURKE (eds.), *Framing Our Past: Canadian Women's History in the Twentieth Century*, Montreal and Kingston, McGill-Queen's University Press, 2001, pp. 22-26, 434-435.

— *The Culture of Catholic Women's Colleges at the University of Toronto 1911-1925*, in: *Canadian Catholic Historical Association Historical Studies*, 70 (2004), pp. 111-130.

— *Educating the Exceptional Child: English-Canadian Women in Religious and Residential Special Education, 1935-1960*, unpublished paper presented at *ISCHE 26: New Education: Genesis and Metamorphoses*, Geneva, 2004.

— *Loretto Academy Niagara (1861-1969): Education under the Rainbow*, in: *Encounters on Education*, 7 (2006), pp. 25-42.

— *Gertrude Lawler and St Joseph's Academy: Alumnae, Advocate and Author*, in: *Canadian Catholic Historical Association Historical Studies*, 72 (2006), pp. 124-141.

— *Sister-Professors: Roman Catholic Women Religious as Academics in English Canada, 1897-1962*, in: P. STORTZ & E.L. PANAYOTIDIS (eds.), *Historical Identities: The Professoriate in Canada*, Toronto, University of Toronto Press, 2006, pp. 207-224.

— *"Sisters Shall not Speak of the Defects": Canadian Women Religious and Youth at Risk 1867-1901*, unpublished paper presented at *ISCHE 29: Children and Youth at Risk*, Hamburg, 2007.

— *Canonizing the Text: Readers, Teaching Manuals and Ontario Women Religious 1867-1920*, in: A. VAN GORP & M. DEPAEPE (eds.), *Auf der Suche nach der wahren Art von Textbüchern* (Beiträge zur historischen und systematischen Schulbuchforschung 7), Bad Heilbrunn, Verlag Julius Klinkhardt, 2008, pp. 119-127.

SMYTH, E. (ed.), *Changing habits. Women's Religious Orders in Canada*, Montreal, Novalis, 2007.

SMYTH, E.M. & WICKS, L.F. (eds.), *Wisdom Raises Her Voice: The Sisters of St. Joseph of Toronto Celebrate 150 Years: An Oral History*, Toronto, Transcontinental Press, 2001.

SOCHIN, M., *"Du Mäglein höre!" Das Höhere Töchterinstitut St. Elisabeth 1935-1994* (Religion - Politik - Gesellschaft in der Schweiz 48), Fribourg, Academic Press, 2007.

SŒUR LOUISE-MARGUERITE (ed.), *Un héritage: réminiscences du Couvent de la rue Rideau et du Collège Bruyère – A Light Rekindled: Reminiscences of Rideau Street Convent and Bruyère College*, Ottawa, Sœurs de la Charité d'Ottawa, 1988.

SONNET, M., *L'éducation des filles au temps des Lumières*, Paris, Cerf, 1987.

SORREL, C., *La République contre les Congrégations: Histoire d'une passion française (1899-1914)*, Paris, Cerf, 2003.

SOURY-LAVERGNE, F., *Chemin d'éducation: sur les traces de Jeanne de Lestonnac 1556-1640*, Chambray-lès-Tours, CLD, 1985.

SOUTHGATE, E., *Remembering School. Mapping Continuities in Power, Subjectivity & Emotion in Stories of School Life*, New York, Peter Lang, 2003.

STANLEY, M., *Women and Education at St. Ann's Academy, Victoria, British Columbia*, online publication (2000): www.pc.gc.ca/dci/rf-ap/ph3/stann/stann_e.asp.

STAPLETON, D., *A Changing of the Guard: The Change of Leadership of Catholic Secondary Schools in Post World War II Victoria*, paper presented at the *AARE [The Australian Association for Research in Education] Conference*, Adelaide, 1998 (available online).

STENGLER, M., *Where to Now? The Story of the Ursuline Sisters of Prelate 1919-2003*, Saskatoon, Saskatchewan, The Ursuline Sisters of Prelate, 2004.

STEWART JR., G.C., *Marvels of Charity: History of American Sisters and Nuns*, Huntington, Our Sunday Visitor, 1994.

STONE, J.F., *L'Application de la loi dans l'Aveyron: les Soeurs de Saint-Joseph*, in: J. LALOUETTE & J-P. MACHELON (eds.*), Les Congrégations hors-la-loi? Autour de la loi du 1er juillet 1901*, Paris, Cerf, 2002, pp. 271-289.

STROBER, M.H. & LANFORD, A.G., *The Feminization of Public School Teaching: Cross-Sectional Analysis, 1850-1880*, in: *Signs: Journal of Women in Culture & Society*, 11 (1986), pp. 212-235.

STRUB, E.M., *Yes, Lord, Always Yes: A Life of Cornelia Connelly 1809 - 1879, Founder of the Society of the Holy Child Jesus*, Rome, Society of the Holy Child Jesus, 2003.

SUÁREZ PAZOS, M., *La reconstrucció de la memòria escolar a través de les autobiografies*, in: *Educació i història: Revista d'història de l'educació*, 9-10 (2006-2007), pp. 40-48.

SUENENS, K. & MARCÉLIS, A.-D., *Vrouwelijke religieuze instituten in België in de negentiende en twintigste eeuw. Een historiografisch overzicht*, in: M. VAN DIJCK, J. DE MAEYER & M.-E. HENNEAU (eds.), *Historiografie en onderzoeksperspectieven van ordes en congregaties op het grondgebied van de Zuidelijke Nederlanden/België*, special issue of *Revue belge de philologie et d'histoire/Belgisch Tijdschrift voor Filologie en Geschiedenis*, 86:4 (2008).

SULLIVAN, M.C., *Catherine McAuley and the Tradition of Mercy*, Dublin, Four Courts Press, 1995.

SULLIVAN, M.C. (ed.), *The Correspondence of Catherine McAuley, 1818-1841*, Dublin, Four Courts Press, 2004.

SYMES, C., unpublished paper presented at the *26th Annual Conference of the Australian & New Zealand History of Education Society*, Brisbane, 1996.

TAGAGE, L.M., *Onderwijscongregaties en vrijheid van vereniging. Een aspect van de schoolstrijd in Limburg, 1857-1859*, in: *Maaslands melange. Opstellen over Limburgs verleden. Dr. P.J.H. Ubachs aangeboden bij gelegenheid van zijn 65ste verjaardag* (Werken uitgegeven door het Limburgs Geschied- en Oudheidkundig Genootschap 14), Maastricht, Limburgs Geschied- en Oudheidkundig Genootschap, 1990, pp. 290-303.

THEOBALD, M., *"Mere Accomplishments?" Melbourne's Early Ladies' Schools Reconsidered*, in: *History of Education Review*, 13 (1984), pp. 15-28 (reprinted in: A. PRENTICE & M.R. THEOBALD (eds.), *Women who Taught: Perspectives on the History of Women and Teaching*, Toronto, University of Toronto Press, 1991, pp. 71-91).

THIATILDE, M. (ed.), *Das Josefshaus in Vreden. 1911 - 2001. 90 Jahre Schwestern Unserer Lieben Frau in Vreden. Erinnerungen und Berichte* (Beiträge des Heimatvereins Vreden zur Landes- und Volkskunde 59), Vreden, Heimatverein Vreden, 2001.

THIAUCOURT, M.R., *Madre Teresa de Saldanha: vida e obra*, Lisboa, Irmãs Dominicanas de Santa Catarina de Sena, 1987.

THIVIERGE, M., *La syndicalisation des institutrices catholiques, 1900-1959*, in: N. FAHMY-EID & M. DUMONT, *Maîtresses de maison, maîtresses d'école: femmes, famille et éducation dans l'histoire du Québec* (Études d'Histoire du Québec), Montreal, Boréal Express, 1983, pp. 171-189.

THOMPSON, M.S., *Review of Ann M.* HARRINGTON, *Creating Community: Mary Frances Clarke and Her Companions (Dubuque: Sisters of Charity - BVM, 2004)*, in: *The Catholic Historical Review*, 92:4 (2006), pp. 695-697.

— *The Yoke of Grace: American Nuns and Social Change, 1808-1917*, Oxford, Oxford University Press, forthcoming.

TIMMERMANS, R., *Het convent van Betlehem. Een half millennium vrouwelijke spiritualiteit en bedrijvigheid*, Leuven, KADOC, 2000.

TITLEY, B., *Heil Mary: Magdalen Asylums and Moral Regulation in Ireland*, in: *History of Education Review*, 35:2 (2006), pp. 1-15.

TOLLEY, K., *"Many Years before the Mayflower": Catholic Academies and the Development of Parish High Schools in the United States, 1727-1925*, in: N. BEADIE & K. TOLLEY (eds.), *Chartered Schools: Two Hundred Years of Independent Academies in the United States, 1727-1925*, New York, Routledge-Falmer, 2002, pp. 304-328.

— *Music Teachers in the North Carolina Education Market, 1800-1840*, in: *Social Science History*, 32:1 (2008), pp. 75-106.

TORRES-SEPTIÉN, V., *Entre Francia y México: las hermanas educadoras de la orden de San José de Lyon*, in: L.E. GALVÁN LAFARGA & O. LÓPEZ PÉREZ (eds.), *Entre imaginarios y Utopías: Historias de maestras*, México, CIESAS-UNAM-PUEG, 2008.

TRIMINGHAM JACK, C., *Sacred Symbols, School Ideology and the Construction of Subjectivity*, in: *Paedagogica Historica*, 34:3 (1998), pp. 771-794.

— *A Moulding Haven? Competing Educational Discourses in an Australian Preparatory School of the Society of the Sacred Heart, 1944-65*, in: *Historical Studies in Education/Revue d'histoire de l'éducation*, 10:1-2 (1998), pp. 116-39.

— *The Lay Sister in Educational History and Memory*, in: *History of Education*, 29:3 (2000), pp. 181-194.

— *Reproducing an English Sensibility: Landscape and Schooling in the Southern Highlands of New South Wales, 1944-1965*, in: *History of Education Review*, 31:2 (2002), pp. 1-15.

— *Growing Good Catholic Girls: Education and Convent Life in Australia*, Melbourne, Melbourne University Press, 2003.

TURIN, Y., *Femmes et religieuses au XIXème siècle: le féminisme 'en religion'*, Paris, Nouvelle Cité, 1989.

UITTO, M.M., *Expectations and contradictions: Teacher-Student Relationships Told in Teacher Memories*, unpublished paper presented at *The European Conference on Educational Research (ECER): From Teaching to Learning?*, Göteborg, 10 September, 2008.

VAN DAMME, O., *Van Spinhuis tot Hogeschool, 1877-1998. 120 jaar normaalschool Gijzegem*, n.p., n.e., 2002.

VAN DER HEIJDEN-ROGIER, N., *Regina Coeli: Klooster en meisjespensionaat in Vught 1903-1971*, Nijmegen, Valkhof Pers, 2002.

VANDERSTRAETEN, R. & PRENEEL, M., *175 jaar Zusters der Christelijke Scholen Vorselaar (1820-1995)*, Vorselaar-Leuven, Zusters der Christelijke Scholen – KADOC, 1996.

VAN DER VEEN, A. & VERHOEVEN, D., *We Agreed to Be Different: Sisters of Charity of Our Lady Mother of Mercy 1960-2000*, Hilversum, Verloren, 2005.

VAN DRENTH, A., *Religious Inspiration and Professionalism in the Care for the 'Feebleminded' in the Netherlands around 1900*, unpublished paper presented at the *Sixth European Social Science History Conference*, Amsterdam, 22-25 March, 2006.

VAN DRENTH, A. & VAN ESSEN, M., *The Ambiguity of Professing Gender: Women Educationists and New Education in the Netherlands (1890-1940)*, in: *Paedagogica Historica*, 44:4 (2008), pp. 379-396.

VAN ESSEN, M., *Kwekeling tussen akte en ideaal: De opleiding tot onderwijzer(es) vanaf 1800*, Amsterdam, SUN, 2006.

VAN ESSEN, M. & ROGERS, R., *Écrire l'histoire des enseignantes. Enjeux et perspectives internationales*, in: *Histoire de l'éducation*, 98 (2003), pp. 5-35 [translation: *Zur Geschichte der Lehrerinnen: Historiographische Herausforderungen und internationale Perspektiven*, in: *Zeitschrift für Pädagogik*, 3 (2006), pp. 319-337].

VAN ESSEN, M. & ROGERS, R. (eds.), *Les enseignantes. Formations, identités, représentations XIXe-XXe siècles*, special issue of *Histoire de l'éducation*, vol. 98, 2003.

VAN GORP, A. (ed.), *Materiële schoolcultuur. Over artefacten als bron in de onderwijsgeschiedenis*, special issue of *Jaarboek voor de geschiedenis van opvoeding en onderwijs*, 2008.

VAN RIJCKEVORSEL, L.M.L., *Een wereld apart. Geschiedenis van het Sacré-Coeur in Nederland van 1848 tot heden*, Hilversum, Verloren, 1996.

VAN ROMPAEY, L., *Strijd voor waardering*, Antwerpen, Garant, 2003.

VAN ROMPAEY, L., DEPAEPE, M. & SIMON, F., *A Different Kind of Activism: the Position of Catholic Women Teachers in their Union (Belgium, 1950-1965)*, in: *Sens Public. Revue internationale - International webjournal.* Dossier: Les femmes dans l'action militante, syndicale et revendicative de 1945 à nos jours (www.sens-public.org/spip.php?article685).

VAN ROMPAEY, L., DEPAEPE, M. & SIMON, F., *Las maestras católicas y la prohibición de matrimonio. Bélgica, 1920-1963*, paper presented at the *15th International Congress of the Asociación de Historiadores Latinoamericanistas Europeos* (AHILA), Leiden, 2008, to be published in a volume on women teachers in Belgium and Mexico (L.E. GALVÁN LAFARGA & F. SIMON (eds.), México, CIESAS).

VAN SETTEN, H. & VAN GERVEN, E., *Met wapperend habijt: Geschiedenis van het huishoudonderwijs van de Ursulinen van Bergen NH, 1925-1990*, Bergen, Bernardus Smeemanstichting, 1992.

VAN VUGT, J., *De geschiedenis van zusters, paters en broeders. Geschiedschrijving over het religieuze leven in Nederland in de laatste twee eeuwen: Resultaten tot nu toe en wensen voor de toekomst*, in: *Jaarboek Katholiek Documentatie Centrum*, 26 (1997), pp. 126-163.

VIÑAO, A., *Review of A. COSTA RICO, Historia da educación e da cultura en Galicia (séculos IV-XX) (Vigo: Edicións Xerais de Galicia, 2004)*, in: *Paedagogica Historica*, 42:3 (2006), pp. 448-449.

VROMEN, S., *Hidden Children of the Holocaust. Belgian Nuns and their Daring Rescue of Young Jews from the Nazis*, New York, Oxford University Press, 2008.

WALCH, T., *The Diverse Origins of American Catholic Education: Chicago, Milwaukee, and the Nation* (The Heritage of American Catholicism 28), New York, Garland, 1988.

— *Parish School: American Catholic Parochial Education from Colonial Times to the Present*, New York, Crossroad, 1996.

WALL, B.M., *"Definite Lines of Influence": Catholic Sisters and Nurse Training Schools, 1890-1920*, in: *Nursing Research*, 50:5 (2001), pp. 314-321.

WALSH, B., *Roman Catholic Nuns in England and Wales 1800-1937: A Social History*, Dublin, Irish Academic Press, 2002.

WATERS, P.M., *The Ursuline Achievement. A Philosophy of Education for Women. St. Angela Merici, the Ursulines and Catholic Education*, North Carlton, Colonna, 1994.

WEIGAND, G., *Die weiblichen Schulorden und die Mädchenbildung*, in: J.G. PRINZ VON HOHENZOLLERN & M. LIEDTKE (eds.), *Der weite Schulweg der Mädchen. Die Geschichte der Mädchenbildung als Beispiel der Geschichte anthropologischer Fehlurteile* (Schriftenreihe zum Bayerischen Schulmuseum Ichenhausen), Bad Heilbrunn, Klinkhardt, 1990, pp. 127-147.

— *Die weiblichen Schulorden*, in: M. LIEDTKE (ed.), *Handbuch der Geschichte des bayerischen Bildungswesens*, Bad Heilbrunn, Klinkhardt, 1991, vol. 1, pp. 605-621.

WHITE, A., *Frost in May*, New York, Dial Press, 1933.

WHITE, C.O., *Maintaining Anglo-Celtic Cultural Hegemony in Saskatchewan: Rev. E.H. Oliver, Provincial Educational Policy, and the German Catholics*, in: *Historical Studies in Education/Revue d'histoire de l'éducation*, 6:2 (1994), pp. 253-279.

WHITELY, M.F., *Annie Leake's Occupation: Development of a Teaching Career, 1858-1886*, in: *Historical Studies in Education/Revue d'histoire de l'éducation*, 4:1 (1992), pp. 97-112.

WILLIAMS, R., *From Isolation to Integration: St Mary's Hall, University of Melbourne, 1918-1968*, in: *History of Education Review*, 27:1 (1998), pp. 19-32.

WOLOSCHUK, T., *A Promise of Redemption: the Soeurs du Bon Pasteur and Delinquent Girls in Winnipeg, 1911-1948*, in: *Manitoba History*, 51 (Feb. 2006), pp. 16-19.

WYNANTS, P., *Les Sœurs de la Providence de Champion et leurs écoles, 1833-1914*, Namur, Presses Universitaires de Namur, 1984.

— *L'instruction des filles pauvres à Chièvres au XIXe siècle*, in: *Annales du Cercle royal d'histoire et d'archéologie d'Ath et de la région et Musée athois*, 50 (1984-1986), pp. 347-349.

— *Comment écrire l'histoire d'une communauté de religieuses enseignantes (XIX-XXe siècle)*, in: *Leodium* 1987, pp. 1-36.

— *La collaboration entre laïcs et religieuses enseignantes en Belgique. Esquisse historique (XIXe-XXe siècles)*, in: *Vie consacrée*, 60:3 (1988), pp. 154-172.

— *Le gouvernement des instituts féminins de vie active au 19e siècle en Belgique*, in: L. COURTOIS et al. (eds.), *Femmes et pouvoirs. Flux et reflux de l'émancipation féminine depuis un siècle* (Recueil des travaux d'histoire et de philologie de l'Université de Louvain 6e série), Louvain-la-Neuve/Paris, 1992, pp. 81-100.

— *Une école congréganiste dans la lutte scolaire: les soeurs de la Providence à Cuesmes, 1859-1895*, in: *Annales du Cercle archéologique de Mons*, 76 (1994), pp. 367-383.

— *La christianisation des campagnes par l'enseignement populaire au XIXe siècle. Étude de cas: les écoles des sœurs de la Providence et de l'Immaculée Conception*, in: *La Christianisation des campagnes. Actes du colloque du CIHEC, 25-27 août 1994*, Brussels/Rome, Institut Historique Belge de Rome, 1996, pp. 543-562.

— *Pour écrire l'histoire d'un établissement d'enseignement congréganiste: orientations de recherche, sources et méthodes (XIXe - XXe siècles)*, in: *Insediamenti e iniziative Salesiane dopo Don Bosco. Saggi di storiografia* (Istituto Storico Salesiano Roma - Studi 9), Roma, LAS, 1996, pp. 17-62.

— *Per la storia di un'istituzione insegnante religiosa: orientamenti di recerca, fonti e metodi (XIX - XX secolo)*, in: *Richerche Storiche Salesiane*, 15:1 (1996), pp. 7-54.

— *Writing the History of a Religious Teaching Institute: Guidelines for Research, Sources and Methods (19th and 20th centuries)*, in: *Journal of Salesian Studies*, 8 (1998), pp. 91-142.

— *Les religieuses de vie active en Belgique et aux Pays-Bas, 19e-20e siècles*, in: *Revue d'Histoire Ecclésiastique*, 95:3 (2000) [= special issue *Deux mille ans d'histoire de l'Église. Bilan et perspectives historiographiques*], pp. 238-256.

— *België en Nederland op gescheiden wegen? Geschiedschrijving van vrouwelijke congregaties 1990-2000*, in: *Trajecta: tijdschrift voor de geschiedenis van het katholiek leven in de Nederlanden*, 11:1 (2002), pp. 65-75.

— *Chronique d'histoire scolaire, 4: Quenast, une école congréganiste au pays des carrières (1874-1914)*, in: *Revue d'histoire religieuse du Brabant wallon*, 19:3 (2005), pp. 175-187.

— *L'influence des Congrégations en Luxembourg belge (1830-1970)*, in: A. NEUBERG (ed.), *Entre vêpres et maraude: L'enfance en Ardenne de 1850 à 1950*, Bastogne, Musée en Piconrue, 2008, pp. 185-204.

YETANO LAGUNA, A., *Congregaciones femeninas de enseñanza fundadas en Cataluña en el siglo XIX*, in: J.-R. AYMES (ed.), *École et Église en Espagne et en Amérique latine: Aspects idéologiques et institutionnels. Actes du colloque de Tours (4-6 décembre 1987)* (Études hispaniques 8-9), Tours, Publications de l'Université de Tours, 1988, pp. 297-307.

ZYMEK, B. & NEGHABIAN, G. (eds.), *Sozialgeschichte und Statistik des Mädchenschulwesens in den deutschen Staaten 1800-1945* (Datenhandbuch zur deutschen Bildungsgeschichte 2.3), Göttingen, Vandenhoeck & Ruprecht, 2005.